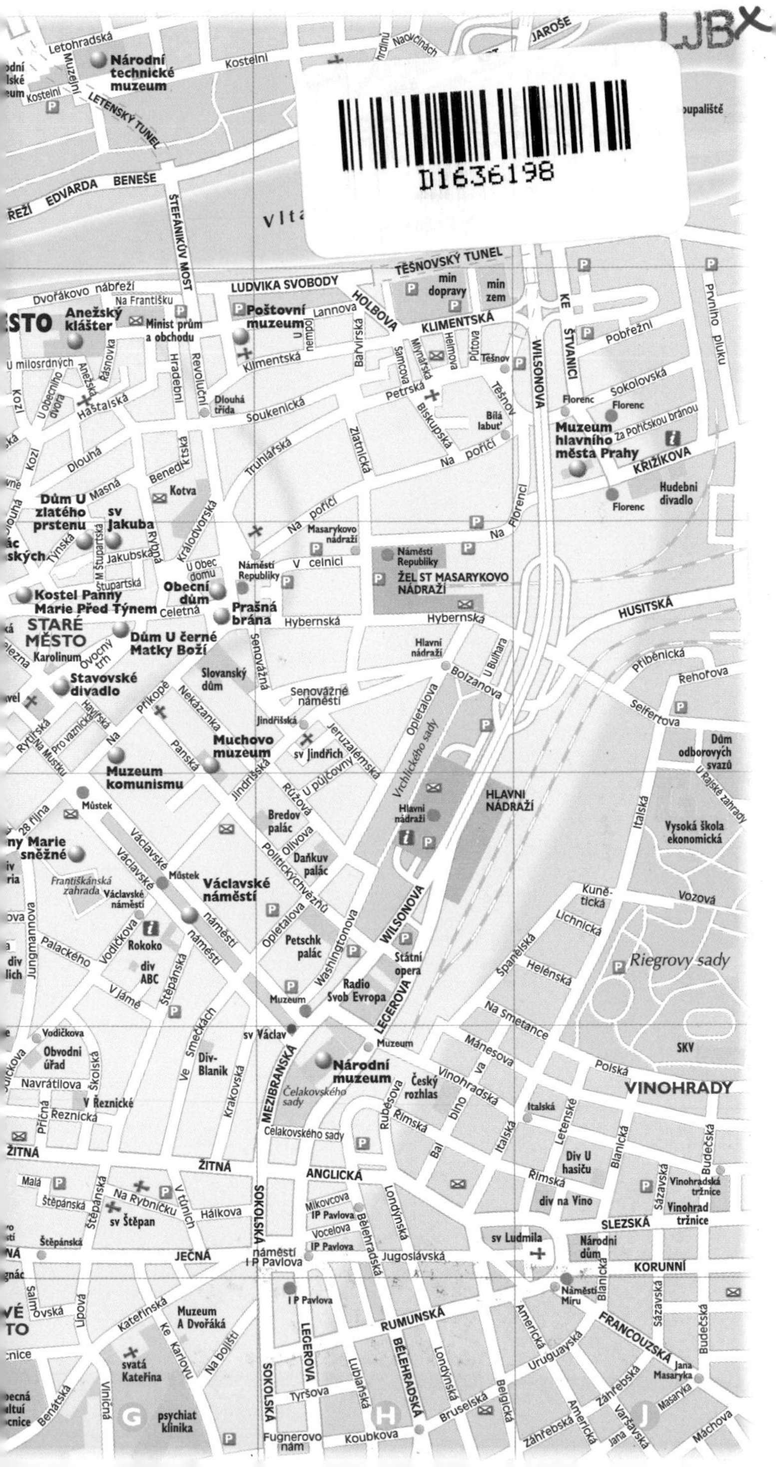

Letohradská
Národní technické muzeum
Kostelní
Muzejní
LETENSKÝ TUNEL
Naovčinách
JAROŠE
D1636198
koupaliště
NÁBŘEŽÍ EDVARDA BENEŠE
ŠTEFÁNIKŮV MOST
Vltava
TĚŠNOVSKÝ TUNEL
Dvořákovo nábřeží
Na Františku
LUDVIKA SVOBODY
min dopravy
min zem
Anežský klášter
Minist prům a obchodu
Poštovní muzeum
Lannova
HOLBOVA
KLIMENTSKÁ
KE ŠTVANICI
Pobřežní
Prvního pluku
U milosrdných
Anežská
Řásnovka
Hradební
Revoluční
Klimentská
Barvířská
Samcova
Mlynářská
Helmova
Půtova
Těšnov
WILSONOVA
Sokolovská
Kozí
U obecního dvora
Haštalská
Dlouhá třída
Soukenická
Petrská
Biskupská
Bílá labuť
Florenc
Muzeum hlavního města Prahy
Za Poříčskou bránou
KŘIŽÍKOVA
Dlouhá
Benediktská
Truhlářská
Zlatnická
Na poříčí
Hudební divadlo
Dům U zlatého prstenu
Masná
sv Jakuba
Kotva
Králodvorská
Týnská
Štupartská
Jakubská
Rybná
Masarykovo nádraží
Na Florenci
Náměstí Republiky
U Obec domu
V celnici
ŽEL ST MASARYKOVO NÁDRAŽÍ
Kostel Panny Marie Před Týnem
Obecní dům
Celetná
Prašná brána
Hybernská
HUSITSKÁ
STARÉ MĚSTO
Dům U černé Matky Boží
Karolinum
Ovocný trh
Senovážná
Hlavní nádraží
U Bulhara
Bolzanova
Příběnická
Řehořova
Stavovské divadlo
Slovanský dům
Senovážné náměstí
Seifertova
Příkopě
Nekázanka
Havířská
Jindřišská
Jeruzalémská
Opletalova
Vrchlického sady
Rytířská
Na Můstku
Pro vaznická
Na
Muchovo muzeum
sv Jindřich
Dům odborových svazů
Panská
U půjčovny
Muzeum komunismu
Růžová
HLAVNÍ NÁDRAŽÍ
U Rajské zahrady
Můstek
28 října
Bredov palác
Olivova
Italská
Vysoká škola ekonomická
Panny Marie sněžné
Václavské
Politických vězňů
Daňkův palác
Františkánská zahrada
Václavské náměstí
Kunětická
Vozová
Lichnická
Jungmannova
Palackého
Vodičkova
Rokoko
div ABC
náměstí
Petschk palác
Washingtonova
WILSONOVA
Státní opera
Španělská
Riegrovy sady
Helénská
V Jámě
Štěpánská
Ve Smečkách
Muzeum
Radio Svob Evropa
LEGEROVA
Na Smetance
sv Václav
Mánesova
Obvodní úřad
Škols ká
Div Blaník
Krakovská
MEZIBRANSKÁ
Národní muzeum
Čelakovského sady
Český rozhlas
Vinohradská
Polská
SKV
VINOHRADY
Navrátilova
V Řeznické
Řeznická
Příčná
Rubešova
Římská
Italská
Blanická
Budečská
Čelakovského sady
ŽITNÁ
Div U hasičů
Letenská
ANGLICKÁ
Londýnská
Sázavská
Vinohradská tržnice
Vinohrad tržnice
Malá
Na Rybníčku
V tůních
Hálkova
Mikovcova
IP Pavlova
Vocelova
sv Štěpán
div na Vinohradech
SLEZSKÁ
sv Ludmila
Národní dům
Štěpánská
JEČNÁ
SOKOLSKÁ
náměstí I P Pavlova
Jugoslávská
Bělehradská
KORUNNÍ
Náměstí Míru
I P Pavlova
Salmovská
Lípová
Kateřinská
Muzeum A Dvořáka
Ke Karlovu
RUMUNSKÁ
Americká
FRANCOUZSKÁ
Na bojišti
svatá Kateřina
Uruguayská
Záhřebská
Jana Masaryka
Benátská
Viničná
psychiat klinika
SOKOLSKÁ
LEGEROVA
Ljublaňská
BĚLEHRADSKÁ
Londýnská
Bruselská
Belgická
Tyršova
Fügnerovo nám
Koubkova
Záhřebská
Americká
Jana Masaryka
Varšavská
Máchova
G
H
J

914.3712 IVO
1421 5324 LJB
Ivory, Michael.

Prague's 25Best

by Michael Ivory

Fodor's Travel Publications
New York • Toronto
London • Sydney • Auckland
www.fodors.com

How to Use This Book

KEY TO SYMBOLS

- Map reference to the accompanying fold-out map
- Address
- Telephone number
- Opening/closing times
- Restaurant or café
- Nearest railway station
- Nearest Metro (subway) station
- Nearest bus route
- Nearest riverboat or ferry stop
- Facilities for visitors with disabilities
- Other practical information
- Further Information
- Tourist information
- Admission charges: Expensive (over 150Kč), Moderate (50–150Kč), and Inexpensive (50Kč or less).
- Major Sight ★ Minor Sight
- Walks
- Excursions
- Shops
- Entertainment and Nightlife
- Restaurants

This guide is divided into four sections

• Essential Prague: an introduction to the city and tips on making the most of your stay.

• Prague by Area: we've broken the city into five areas, and recommended the best sights, shops, entertainment venues, nightlife and restaurants in each one. Suggested walks help you to explore on foot.

• Where to Stay: the best hotels, whether you're looking for luxury, budget or something in between.

• Need to Know: the info to make your trip run smoothly, including getting about by public transport, weather tips, emergency phone numbers and useful websites.

Navigation In the Prague by Area chapter, we've given each area its own colour, which is also used on the locator maps throughout the book and the map on the inside front cover.

Maps The fold-out map accompanying this book is a comprehensive street plan of Prague. The grid on this fold-out map is the same as the grid on the locator maps within the book. We've given grid references within the book for each sight and listing.

Contents

Introducing Prague

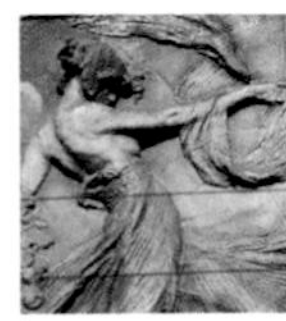

Nearly two decades after the Velvet Revolution, Prague is the short-break destination of choice for millions of visitors. Its rich culture and a miraculously preserved architectural heritage more than meet their expectations.

Built on both banks of the Vltava and with a castle atop a rocky spur, Prague is a glorious fusion of nature and architecture. It is the very image of what a capital city was before the onset of the industrial age. Woods and orchards sweep down to the water's edge, while the skyline is pierced by myriad towers and steeples. Buildings of every era stand side by side, from burgher's house to baroque palace, from art nouveau apartment block to Cubist café. The historic hub is compact enough to be easily explored on foot (though the excellent public transport system can help take the strain).

In the 1990s, when the world started to come to a Prague that it had ignored for so long, many locals felt excluded, resentful that the city had been taken over by foreigners. Times have changed; while tourism has become a mainstay of the economy, increasingly prosperous Czechs have begun to reclaim their territory. Sleek modern hotels and daring fusion restaurants are no longer just the preserve of visitors, and bars and cafes are filled with stylishly attired young locals.

Prague's guests are better catered for than ever before; as well as an expanding choice of places to sleep and eat, once-dusty museums are modernizing, and glittering new attractions include a museum for the city's most famous literary son, Franz Kafka. Beware of Prague's embrace! It was Kafka who warned of Prague that 'this little mother has claws', and once in her grasp you may find it difficult to leave.

Facts + Figures

- **Prague's population is 1.15 million.**
- **Czechs drink an average of 160 litres (338 pints) of beer per person per year.**
- **The city has 10,000 works of art and protected objects.**

THE 1,000-YEAR FLOOD

The usually tranquil Vltava can present another, fiercer face, as in 1890, when its waters rose and swept away three arches of Charles Bridge. But the worst-ever flood came in August 2002, when whole districts were under water, thousands of people had to be evacuated and billions of crowns of damage were caused.

PRAGUE PEOPLE

Half of Prague's 1,150,000 citizens live in *paneláks*, the high-rise, prefabricated apartment blocks of Communist times that form a ring around the city. Those that can afford it are opting to move to the greener surroundings and fresher air in the countryside beyond, creating a commuting culture that hardly existed before.

VISITORS TO THE RESCUE

Even before Communism, Prague was an important manufacturing base, and the totalitarian regime promoted industries of all kinds. Since 1989 tourism has taken over from industry as the city's big earner, helping to keep unemployment at virtually nil compared with worrying levels in the rest of the country.

A Short Stay in Prague

DAY 1

Morning Start on the steps in front of the Národní Muzeum (▷ 48) with a view down Václavské náměstí. Go through the underpass to the statue of Good King Wenceslas, then walk down the square. Look into the Lucerna Passage and admire mischievous artist David Černý's zany take on the Wenceslas statue. At the foot of the square head west along 28 října and Národní třída to catch the No. 22 (Bílá Hora) or 23 (Malovanka) tram from the stop behind the Tesco store. Enjoy the ride across the River Vltava (▷ 52), through Malá Strana and up to Pražský hrad. Linger in the courtyards, looking into the Old Royal Palace, Katedrála sv Víta (▷ 68) and Golden Lane. Descend to Malá Strana via steep Nerudova (▷ 89), marvel at the baroque interior of Chrám sv Mikuláše (▷ 84), then go through the lanes to tranquil Kampa Island.

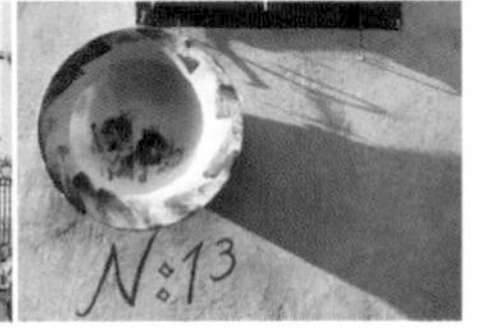

Lunch Enjoy lunch in the riverside restaurant attached to the Muzeum Kampa (▷ 89).

Afternoon Cross the Vltava via Karlův most (▷ 28) and lose yourself among the labyrinthine lanes of the Old Town before finding your way to Staroměstské náměstí (▷ 32), making sure that you are there on the hour to see the Astronomical Clock in action.

Dinner Tuck into a substantial Czech feast of duck, cabbage and dumplings at one of the Kolkovna group's superpubs, such as Celnice (▷ 61).

Evening Continue your night out in one of the city's traditional pubs such as U Fleků (▷ 62) or Černý Orel (▷ 93).

DAY 2

Morning Board tram 22 or 23 at a convenient point and ride to the Pohořelec stop. Admire the halls of Strahovský klášter (▷ 74) then soak up the glorious city panorama while sipping coffee on the terrace of the Bellavista restaurant (▷ 80). Catch the carillon at the Loreta (▷ 70) and time your arrival at the western entrance of the castle to watch the midday changing of the guard. Go down to Malá Strana via Nové zámecké schody (New Castle Steps) and walk through Valdštejnský palác (▷ 88) and its garden to the little riverside park at the end of Mánes Bridge, from where there is an unusual view across the river to Charles Bridge and the Old Town.

Lunch Enjoy a meal at the Hergetova cihelna restaurant (▷ 93).

Afternoon Retrace your steps to Malostranská station and travel two stops to Müstek. On emerging from the station, walk northeastwards along Na Příkopě, one of the city's foremost shopping streets, to the Prašná brána/Powder Tower (▷ 36) and the Obecní dům/Municipal House (▷ 30) After a conducted tour of the fabulous art nouveau interiors of the Municipal House, relax with coffee and cakes in its sumptuous café. Afterwards, go a short distance along Celetná, admiring the Black Madonna building before turning right through a passageway to Štupártská and Malá Štupartská, then beneath the archway into Týn Court. Cross Old Town Square to the Pařížská shopping boulevard and Josefov (▷ 26), visiting the Old/New Synagogue and the Old Jewish Cemetery.

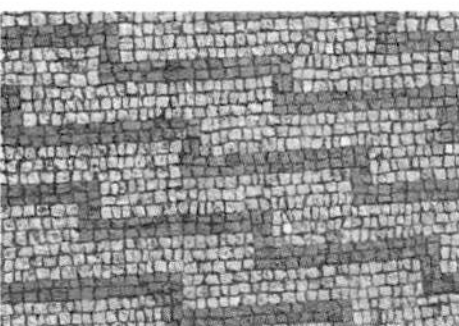

Dinner Dine at a restaurant with a view—Petřínské terasy (▷ 94).

Evening Be thrilled by opera or ballet in the Národní divadlo (▷ 60).

Top 25

Anežský klášter ▷ 24 St Agnes's Convent is the home of fine works of medieval sculpture.

Bazilika a klášter sv Jiři ▷ 67 St George's Basilica has an austere Romanesque interior.

Chrám sv Mikuláše (Malá Strana) ▷ 84 An interior unsurpassed for sheer extravagance.

Josefov ▷ 26 The synagogues and cemetery at an evocative site of Jewish heritage.

Karlův most ▷ 28 This medieval bridge is lined with statues of gesticulating baroque saints.

Katedrála sv Víta ▷ 68 This cathedral demonstrates the history of Christianity in the country.

Loreta ▷ 70 This gorgeous baroque building, a place of pilgrimage, is famous for its carillon.

Malostranské náměsti ▷ 86 This square is at the heart of Prague's best-preserved historic quarter.

Muchovo muzeum ▷ 46 Dedicated to the master of art nouveau.

Národní divadlo ▷ 47 The National Theatre is splendid for classical music, opera and ballet.

Národní muzeum ▷ 48 The museum is modernizing the presentation of its vast collections.

Národní technické muzeum ▷ 102 Wonders include old-timers of road and rail.

Obecní dům ▷ 30 Extravagant examples of art nouveau architecture and interior design.

Petřin ▷ 87 The woods, orchards and open spaces here bring the countryside into the heart of the city.

Pražský hrad ▷ 72 Prague Castle is the citadel of Czech culture and history.

Staroměstské náměstí ▷ 32 The square houses the medieval Tyn Church and the Town Hall tower.

Šternberský palác ▷ 71 A fitting setting for the nation's fine European Old Master paintings.

Strahovský klášter ▷ 74 The towers of Strahov Monastery overlook the city.

Vyšehrad ▷ 49 The city's second citadel offers wonderful views plus insights into Czech history.

Vltava Boat Trip ▷ 52 A leisurely river cruise is a good way to absorb the city's unique atmosphere.

Veletržní palác ▷ 100 An icon of Modernist architecture with an outstanding collection of art.

Valdštejnský palác ▷ 88 Prague's most ostentatious palace, with a superb formal garden.

Václavské náměstí ▷ 50 Broad boulevard with the famous statue of St. Wenceslas on his horse.

Uměleckoprůmyslové muzeum ▷ 34 A treasure house of glass, ceramics, furniture and more.

Trojský zámek ▷ 98 Troja Château is a noble out-of-town residence set in formal gardens.

This is a quick guide to the Top 25, which are described in more detail later. Here they are listed alphabetically, and the tinted background shows the area they are in.

Shopping

It's increasingly hard for visitors to escape uniformity and find local products worth taking home. Thanks to their long tradition as craftsmen and artisans, however, the Czechs have plenty to offer. Along with crystal and garnets, don't overlook the herbal liqueur Becherovka, blue onion porcelain and art books.

Antiques

Antiques stores, found under signs reading *starožítnictví*, *bazar* or *vetešnictví* (junk shop), contain many treasures: Quality paintings, kitchenware, jewellery and linens can be found at reasonable prices. Many bazaars specialize in old cameras, clocks and other mechanical devices.

Fashion

A number of Czech fashion designers are making a name for themselves and have opened successful boutiques where you can find original pieces at a fraction of what you'd pay at home for a similar-quality item. Most of these shops are concentrated on a few streets north of Old Town Square—Dlouhá, Dušní and V Kolkovně. Fashionable international names line nearby Pařížska, but don't expect bargains there.

Books

Considering the Czechs' contribution to art, architecture and photography, it's not

SPA TREATS

A whole culture has grown up around Czech spa towns. Re-create this atmosphere at home by strolling about, sipping water from a porcelain cup with a built-in straw and sipping spa waters, or *oplátky*. The cups can be found cheaply in antiques shops. Round off your cure with a shot of Becherovka, the herbal liqueur developed by a spa doctor in Karlovy Vary in 1807. It's said to be especially good for stomach ailments.

From antique books to toys and painted eggs, Prague has plenty of good souvenir choices

While in Prague you'll find that the Grand Café's cakes (above) are irresistible. Enjoy!

surprising that handsome coffee-table books devoted to subjects such as Czech cubism, avant-garde photography and the art nouveau movement are popular.

Glassware

Glass and crystal, of course, are ubiquitous, and the sheer number of shops and variety of products can be overwhelming. But Czech crystal is famous for a reason and should not be overlooked. Stick to shops affiliated with just one or two manufacturers that focus primarily on tableware and larger individual pieces and you're likely to take home something of real quality. Look for hand-blown, hand-cut lead crystal produced by names such as Moser and Sklo Bohemia, and Desná for art deco.

Souvenirs

Much of what is sold in the tourist areas has no relation to local traditions or culture: Russian dolls, Polish amber and non-Czech crystal. Lace tablecloths are more likely to have been made by Russian experts. If any of these products catches your eye and doesn't break the bank there's nothing wrong in buying it—but if your heart is set on a real Czech souvenir, keep looking.

NOT ALL GARNETS ARE CREATED EQUAL

The Czechs have been mining garnets for centuries. Said to bring vitality and cure depression, the Bohemian variety of garnet is not found anywhere else in the world. They are a deep, rich red known as 'dove's blood' and the settings typically feature many small garnets clustered together. Most garnet jewellery is made by the cooperative Granát Turnov and sold in factory stores and by authorized dealers with a stamp of approval. However, a fair amount of what is sold in Prague as Bohemian garnets is actually made from almandines or other stones from Italy and elsewhere. Showy gold pieces set with large, brownish stones are not Bohemian garnets.

Shopping by Theme

Whether you're looking for a department store, a quirky boutique, or something in between, you'll find it all in Prague. On this page shops are listed by theme. For a more detailed write-up, see the individual listings in Prague by Area.

ANTIQUES

Ahasver Antiques (▷ 92)
Alma Antique (▷ 38)
Dorotheum (▷ 38)
Hodinářství Václav Matouš (▷ 58)

ARTS AND CRAFTS

Galerie Peithner-Lichtenfels (▷ 39)
Moser (▷ 58)

BOOKS

Academia (▷ 57)
Anagram (▷ 38)
Antikvariát Pařížská (▷ 38)
Big Ben Bookshop (▷ 38)
Gambra (▷ 79)
Globe Bookstore and Coffeehouse (▷ 57)
Hatle Antikvariát (▷ 58)
Kožešiny Kubín (▷ 92)
Knihkupectví U Černé Matki Božé (▷ 39)
Kiwi (▷ 58)
Matky Boží (▷ 39)
Palác Knih Luxor (▷ 58)
U Zlaté Čiše (▷ 92)

COSMETICS

Botanicus (▷ 38)

FASHION

Elazar (▷ 57)
Ivana Follová Art & Fashion (▷ 39)
Liska (▷ 39)
Myslivost (▷ 58)
Pavla A Olga (▷ 92)

FOOD AND WINE

Cellarius (▷ 57)
Country Life (▷ 38)
Culinaria (▷ 38)
Dům vín České Republiky (▷ 38)
Fruits de France (▷ 57)
Havelská/V Kotcích (▷ 39)
Hynek Cibulka Uzenřství (▷ 39)
Zlatý Kříž (▷ 58)

GLASS

Art Deco (▷ 38)
Celetná Crystal (▷ 38)
Galerie Pyramida (▷ 57)

HANDICRAFTS AND SOUVENIRS

Manufaktura (▷ 39)
Museum Shop (▷ 79)
Tupesy (▷ 39)
Zlatá Ulička (▷ 79)

JEWELLERY

Granát (▷ 39)
Pražské Starožitnosti (▷ 58)

MUSIC

Bontonland Koruna (▷ 57)
Cdmusic.cz (▷ 79)
Moser (▷ 39)

PHOTOGRAPHY

Centrum Fotoškoda (▷ 57)

STORES

Bílá Labuť (▷ 57)
Kotva (▷ 39)
Tesco (▷ 58)

TOYS AND GAMES

Classic Model (▷ 38)
Daddy Toys (▷ 57)
Obchod S Loutkami (▷ 92)

Prague by Night

There are a variety of night-time activities: traditional dancing, classical music, clubs and pubs.

Drinking in Prague

Prague has no shortage of hip dance clubs and trendy bars, but for most Czechs, the best nights are spent in a pub. No visitor should pass up the opportunity to taste an expertly poured Pilsner or Budvar at the long wooden tables of a typical Czech pub. An alternative is the *vinárna* (wine bar). A *vinárna* can be a restaurant, but more typically is a small establishment, sometimes with standing room only, offering inexpensive Czech or Slovak wines, often of surprisingly good quality.

All That Jazz

Czechs are known for being a musical nation and on any given night there are a variety of concerts on offer, from local modern jazz fixtures like Emil Viklický to touring Balkan gypsy bands to performances of Dvořák and Smetana. Postage-stamp jazz joints abound in downtown and larger venues like Malostranská beseda, the Roxy (▷ 40) and Akropolis book an eclectic mix of acts.

Staying Out Late

Night owls thirsty for a cocktail should head for the bars just north of Old Town Square. Another district that's home to hip bars and clubs is located behind the National Theatre. Of course you can always take a romantic stroll and view the floodlit castle from the blissfully empty Charles Bridge.

WHAT'S ON

The best source of information for English-language readers about what's on in Prague is probably the tabloid 'Night and Day' section of the weekly newspaper *Prague Post*.
Tickets for events can be obtained at box offices (which may be less expensive) or through Ticketpro (☎ 234 704 234; www.ticketpro.cz) or Bohemia Ticket (☎ 224 227 832; www.bohemiaticket.cz).

Eating Out

Traditional Czech cuisine is substantial, based on meat, dumplings, soups and rich sauces. Fruit and vegetables are relegated to minor roles, but there are plenty of sweet things, including delicious cakes and pastries, among them irresistible strudels. Pork is the preferred meat, served in a variety of ways, of which the most challenging is a whole knuckle with mustard and horseradish. You should sample at least one meal of this kind, perhaps in one of the updated beerhalls like Celnice (▷ 61) or U Pinkasů (▷ 62).

International and Fast Food Dining

Virtually every taste is well catered for, from American to vegetarian, via French and fusion. Only at the upper end of the range do prices approach levels common in other capital cities. Fast food has arrived, but rather than eating in pizza and burger establishments with familiar names, do as the locals do and feast on a wonderfully greasy sausage served from a stall in the street.

Drinks

Heavy meals are best washed down with a glass or three of beer, preferably draught. The world's wines are widely available in Prague, though you should at least try a white wine from Bohemia or Moravia and perhaps a red from Slovakia. The traditional aperitif is Becherovka from Karlsbad, while local spirits include ginlike borovička and fiery plum brandy, slivovice.

WHERE TO DINE

With a wide choice of places to eat, it's worthwhile choosing somewhere with a distinctive setting, of which there are many. You can dine in the stately ambience of an historic palace, sit at a table with a stunning view over spires and rooftops or the swiftly flowing Vltava, or enjoy a hearty repast beneath the vaults of a medieval cellar.

From grand old eateries to modern-day sandwich outlets you will find a good range of cuisine.

Restaurants by Cuisine

There are restaurants to suit all tastes and budgets in Prague. On this page they are listed by cuisine. For a more detailed description of each restaurant, see Prague by Area.

AMERICAN

Bohemia Bagel (▷ 93)
Red Hot & Blues (▷ 42)

ASIAN

Orange Moon (▷ 41)

CAFÉS

Au Gourmand (▷ 41)
Café Ebel (▷ 93)
Café Louvre (▷ 61)
Café Savoy (▷ 93)
Globe Bookstore & Coffeehouse (▷ 57)
Kavárna Evropa (▷ 61)
Lobkowicz Palace (▷ 80)
Slavia (▷ 42)
Velryba (▷ 62)
U zlaté studně (▷ 80)

CZECH

Allegro (▷ 41)
Celnice (▷ 61)
Klub Architektů (▷ 41)
Kolkovna (▷ 41)
Hybernia (▷ 61)
Lví dvůr (▷ 80)
Novoměstský pivovar (▷ 61)
Petřínské terasy (▷ 94)
Plzeňská restaurace (▷ 41)
Pod křídlem (▷ 62)
Potrefena Husá (▷ 41–42)
Sovovy mlýny (▷ 94)
Století (▷ 42)
U Císařů (▷ 80)
U Kalicha (▷ 62)
U Medvídků (▷ 42)
U modré Kachničky (▷ 94)
U modré Kachničky II (▷ 42)
U Pinkasů (▷ 62)
U Šuterů (▷ 62)
U zlaté hrušky (▷ 80)

EASTERN EUROPEAN

Vikárka (▷ 80)
Zvonice (▷ 62)
Gitanes (▷ 93)
Hungarian Grotto (▷ 93–94)

FISH

Alcron (▷ 61)
Kampa Fish (▷ 94)
Rybí trh (▷ 42)
Triton (▷ 62)

FRENCH

Chez Marcel (▷ 41)
La Perle de Prague (▷ 62)
U Malířů (▷ 94)

INTERNATIONAL

Alchymist (▷ 93)
Barok (▷ 41)
Bellavista (▷ 80)
Coda (▷ 93)
David (▷ 93)
Hergetova Cihelna (▷ 93)
Hot (▷ 61)
Kampa Park (▷ 94)
Pálffy palác (▷ 94)
Zahrada v opěre (▷ 62)

ITALIAN

Amici Miei (▷ 41)
Cicala (▷ 61)

KOSHER

King Solomon (▷ 41)

PUBS

Černý Orel (▷ 93)
U Fleků (▷ 62)
U kocoura (▷ 94)
U Pářašutistů (▷ 62)
U Vejvodů (▷ 42)

VEGETARIAN

Country Life (▷ 41)
Govinda Vegetarian Club (▷ 61)

If You Like...

However you'd like to spend your time in Prague, these top suggestions should help you tailor your ideal visit. Each sight or listing has a fuller write-up in Prague by Area.

UNUSUAL ANTIQUES

Enhance your appreciation of Bohemian glass and porcelain by studying the stunning exhibits at the Uměleckoprůmyslové muzeum (UPM – Applied Arts Museum ▷ 34).
Avoid the souvenir shops along the tourist trail, and look instead at the Dorotheum (▷ 38).
Bargain at reputable antiques establishments such as Alma Antique (▷ 38).

Glassware and antiques are worth seeking out in Prague.

HISTORIC HOTELS

Look for luxurious lodgings behind the baroque façade of the Hotel Adria (▷ 112) in Wenceslas Square.
Take up residence in the Mandarin Oriental Hotel (▷ 112), an exquisitely sensitive conversion of a 14th-century monastery in the quietest part of Malá Strana.
Luxuriate in the stylish K&K Central Hotel (▷ 112), a jewel of art nouveau architecture and interior design.

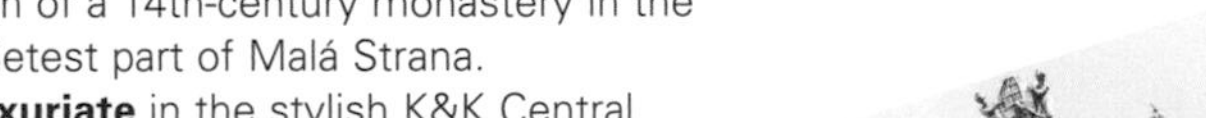

DINING WITH A VIEW

See the incomparable view of Prague from the terrace of the Bellavista (▷ 80).
Take the elevator to the top of Frank Gehry's 'Dancing Building' overlooking the Vltava, and enjoy the French cuisine of La Perle de Prague (▷ 62).
Enjoy countrified views from Petřínské terasy, perched amid the greenery of Petřín Hill (▷ 94).
Gaze down over Malá Strana from U zlaté studně (▷ 80), tucked away against the Castle ramparts.

Try local fare to get a true taste of the city.

CZECH COOKING

Tuck into the updated traditional dishes on offer in the café/bar, ground-floor restaurant, garden terrace or deep cellar of the Hybernia (▷ 61).

Sate your appetite with hearty Bohemian fare at U Pinkasů (▷ 62), and wash it down with well-kept Pilsner Urquell.

Enjoy duck and dumplings at Kolkovna (▷ 41), a refined version of the classic Czech pub.

BEING PAMPERED

Relax in the wellness area of a five-star hotel (some of which are open to non-guests), none of which outclasses the superb spa that is part of the Mandarin Oriental Hotel (▷ 112).

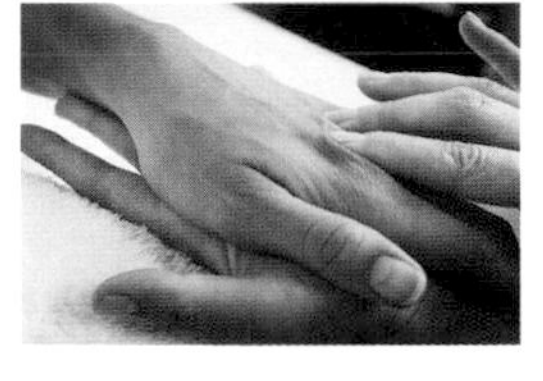

Find your way to the Sabai Studio in the Slovanský dům arcade, and submit to the attentions of qualified massage therapists, whose treatments have been developed in Thailand for over a thousand years.

Find your own way to relax—at a spa or enjoying a massage.

GREAT JAZZ

Force your way into the cramped basement of U malěho Glena (▷ 92) to soak up some of the city's best jazz.

Storm the great stronghold of Czech jazz, the Reduta (▷ 60)—The Redoubt—which has enjoyed presidential patronage on more than one occasion.

Ignore the misleading name ('The Old Lady'), hot sessions are a nightly rule at Jazz Club U staré paní (▷ 40).

Live music—be it jazz, traditional or contemporary can be enjoyed in a variety of venues.

KEEPING THE KIDS HAPPY

There are activities to involve your children

Take them up to the top of Petřín Hill in the funicular and watch them split their sides at the distorting mirrors of the Bludiště (▷ 87).

Exploring the city by tram can be exciting for kids used to being ferried around in cars. Bear in mind that you get the best views by standing right at the back.

Visit the Výstaviště (▷ 104), whose attractions include a funfair, then continue out of town to the Zoo.

GETTING UP HIGH

Brave the high-speed elevator of the Televizní vysílač/TV Tower in Žižkov for a view extending over 100km (62 miles).

Toil up the endless steps of the tower of Chram sv Mikuláše (▷ 84) and emerge high above the red rooftops of Malá Strana.

Climb toward heaven via the winding staircase of the south tower of Katedrála sv Víta (▷ 68) for a panorama otherwise enjoyed only by angels.

SEEING THE CITY IN STYLE

Take to the water for a pleasure cruise along the Vltava (▷ 52).

Hop aboard a vintage tram (▷ 119) for a nostalgic trip along the tracks.

Sit in a stylish Škoda or other oldtimer and be driven round the sights.

Take to the waters to see the city from the Vltava river. Boat trips head downstream and most pass under five bridges. In fine weather you can opt to sit outside as you view the city from a different angle.

Prague by Area

STARÉ MĚSTO

NOVÉ MĚSTO

HRADČANY

MALÁ STRANA

FARTHER AFIELD

Within the Old Town's labyrinth of lanes is the greatest concentration of Prague's historic buildings, plus intriguing shops, bars and restaurants. Close by is Josefov, the historic Jewish quarter.

5
6
7
8
9
D
E
F
Čechův most
Dvořákovo
sv Šimon a Juda
Kozí
náměstí Curieových
Dušní
U milosrdných
Dvořákovo nábřeží
Právnická fakulta
UK
Pařížská
P
El Krásnohorské
Bílkova
Břehová
padu
ČVUT Konzerv
17 listo
Na rejdišti
U st. hř
Dušní
Vězeňská
Uměleckoprůmyslové muzeum
P
bitova
Staronová Synagóga
V Kolkovně
Mánesův most
Rudolfinum
P
Široká
Pařížská
Dlouhá
Alšův nábřeží
JOSEFOV
Maiselova
Jáchymova
Palác Kinských
Staroměstská
Kaprova
Valentinská
Žatecká
Exposice Franze Kafky
Staroměstské náměstí
Křižovnická
Veleslavín
Platnéřská
Mariánské náměstí
Kostel Panny Marie Před Týnem
Karlův most
Staroměstská radnice
Karlův most
Klementinum
Husova
Malé náměstí
Železná
Křižovnické náměstí
Melantrichova
Kožná
Muzeum loutkářských kultur
Karlova
Dům pánů z Kunštátu a Podebřad
Muzeum Bedřicha Smetany
Liliová
sv Havel
Anenska
Řetězová
Michalská
sv Jiljí
Betlémská kaple
Husova
Jilská
Havelská
V Kotcích
Rytířská
Karlovy lázně
nábřeží
stříbrná
Náprstkova
Vejvodova
Smetanovo
Skořepka
Perlová
Vltava
0
250 m
0
250 yds

Vltava
nábřeží
Anežský klášter
Klášterská
Řásnovka
Anežská
dvora
Haštalská
Hradební
Dlouhá třída
Soukenická
Dlouhá
Masná
Benediktská
Revoluční
Truhlářská
Kotva
Dům U zlatého prstenu
sv Jakuba
Týnská
Malá Štupartská
Jakubská
Rybná
Králodvorská
Na poříčí
U Obec domu
Náměstí Republiky
P
Štupartská
Obecní dům
Prašná brána
STARÉ MĚSTO
Celetná
Hybernská
Dům U černé Matky Boží
Ovocný trh
Karolinum
Stavovské divadlo
Na Příkopě
Havířská
Provaznická
Na Můstku
G
H

Anežský klášter

HIGHLIGHTS

- *Madonna of Vyšehrad* painting
- *Madonna and Child* sculpture from Český Krumlov
- Panel paintings by the Master of Vyšší Brod
- Portraits of saints by Master Theodoricus
- *Christ on the Mount of Olives* by the Třeboň Master
- Votive altarpiece from Zlíchov
- *Madonna of Poleň,* Cranach the Elder
- Vaulted medieval cloister
- Church of St. Francis (concert hall)
- Church of the Holy Saviour

St. Agnes's Convent, the city's most venerable Gothic complex, shelters in a quiet precinct of the Old Town. Once earmarked for destruction, it is now the fitting home for one of the country's most distinctive galleries.

Canonized Czech Agnes was a 13th-century princess, sister of Wenceslas I and founder of a convent of Poor Clares here. In its glory days St. Agnes's was a mausoleum for the royal family, but was it sacked by the Hussites in the 15th century. In 1782, it was closed down by Joseph II, and became slum housing until city authorities decided to raze it in the 1890s, only relenting when faced with bitter public protest. The convent was slowly restored, and, in November 1989, days before the Communist

Church of Sv Frantisek (St. Francis of Assisi) in Anežský klášter (left); the altarpiece called Resurrection *by the Master of the Trebon, c.1380, in Anežský klášter (middle); Church of Sv Salvator (Holy Saviour, below)*

regime ended, Agnes was made a saint. An auspicious omen?

Medieval masterpieces The convent now displays the National Gallery's collection of medieval art from Czech lands and nearby. The magnificent works show the extraordinary achievements in the fine arts in Bohemia, above all during the reigns of Emperor Charles IV and his successors. Prague's court artists fused Italian, French and Flemish influences in a manner all their own, pointing towards the late-Gothic style that flourished in Europe.

Look down The vista to St. Agnes's Convent from Letná Plain on the far side of the Vltava gives a fascinating overview of this medieval riverside complex of buildings.

THE BASICS

www.ngprague.cz
G6
U Milosrdných 17
221 879 111; 224 810 628
Tue–Sun 10–6
Náměstí Republiky
Tram 17 (Právnická fakulta stop) or tram 5, 14 (Dlouhá třída stop)
Fair
Moderate

Josefov

HIGHLIGHTS

- Vine carving in entrance portal
- Tombstone of Rabbi Loew (*c.*1525–1609)

TIP

- Remember that the Old/New Synagogue is still a place of worship for the Jewish community, and that men should cover their heads, both here and in the cemetery (paper *kippah* are available).

With its synagogues and age-old cemetery, Josefov is one of the most evocative sites of Jewish heritage anywhere, testimony to a world that lasted for a thousand years until brought to an end by the brutal Nazi occupation.

Ghetto memories Josefov owes its name to the liberal Emperor Josef II, who emancipated the Jews in 1781, but the ghetto itself dates from the 13th century, when its high walls kept its inhabitants in and their Christian neighbours out. Over time it produced many remarkable characters, foremost among them, learned Rabbi Loew, creator of that archetypal man-made monster, the Golem. The ghetto's warren of twisting lanes and dark courtyards was swept away in the late 19th century, when only

Clockwise from left: Maiselova Synagoga; Spanelkska Synagoga or Spanish Synagogue; view along Kaprova Street; art nouveau detail on Kaprova street; statue of a walking headless figure with Franz Kafka; art nouveau apartments; the emblem of the Prague Jewish Community (replica) in the Maiselova Synagoga

its synagogues, cemetery and rococo Town Hall were spared. The Nazis expelled Prague's Jews to the prison town of Terezín and then to Auschwitz. Some of the valuables they stole from Jewish communities all over Bohemia and Moravia are now on display in the synagogues.

The Old/New Synagogue With its pointed brick gable and atmospheric interior, the Gothic synagogue of 1275 is the oldest building of its kind north of the Alps, a compelling reminder of the age-old intertwining of Jewish and Christian culture in Europe.

Old Jewish Cemetery The total number laid to rest beneath the dappled shade of the tall trees may amount to 12,000, laid on top of one another, up to 12 deep in places.

THE BASICS

F6/7

Cemetery: enter through Pinkas Synagogue, Siroka 3

Prague Jewish Museum: 224 819 456; www.jewishmuseum.cz

Jewish Museum: Apr–Oct Sun–Fri 9–6; rest of year 9–4.30. Closed Jewish holidays. Old/New Synagogue: Sun–Thu 9.30–5, Fri 9–4

Staroměstska

Fair

Cemetery/museums: expensive. Old/New Synagogue: moderate

Karlův most

HIGHLIGHTS

- Old Town Bridge Tower
- Malá Strana Bridge Tower (viewpoint)
- Nepomuk statue with bronze relief panels
- Bruncvík (Roland column) to southwest
- Statue of St. John of Matha
- Bronze crucifix with Hebrew inscription
- Statue of St. Luitgard (by Braun)

TIP

- To experience a non-crowded Charles Bridge you need to get there early in the morning, even out of season.

Any time is right to visit Charles Bridge, the magnificent medieval crossing over the Vltava. Enjoy the hucksters, then enjoy the almost sinister dusk, when sculpted saints on the parapets gesticulate against the darkening sky.

Gothic overpass For centuries Karlův most was Prague's only bridge, built on the orders of Emperor Charles IV in the 14th century. It's a triumph of Gothic engineering, with 16 massive sandstone arches carrying it more than 490m (534 yards) from the Old Town to soar across the Vltava River and Kampa Island to touch down near the heart of Malá Strana. It is protected by sturdy timber cutwaters and guarded at both ends by towers; the eastern face of the Old Town Bridge Tower is richly ornamented.

Clockwise from left: people passing artists and vendors on Charles Bridge; statues line the bridge; the Castle with the bridge in front; detail of the clock tower of the Naprstek Museum, seen from the bridge; St. John Nepomuk (patron saint of bridges) with his five-star halo; looking along the bridge.

Its opposite number has by a smaller tower, once part of the earlier Judith Bridge.

Starry saint Charles Bridge has always been much more than a river crossing. Today's traders succeed earlier merchants and stall-holders, and tournaments, battles and executions have all been held on the bridge. The heads of the Protestants executed in 1621 in Old Town Square were displayed here. Later that century the bridge was beautified with baroque sculptures, including the statue of St. John Nepomuk. Falling foul of the king, this unfortunate cleric was pushed off the bridge in a sack. As his body bobbed in the water, five stars danced on the surface. Nepomuk hence became the patron saint of bridges, and is always depicted with his starry halo.

THE BASICS

E7

Staroměstská

Tram 12, 22, 23 to Malostranské náměstí

Good

Bridge free

Obecní dům

Exterior and interior views of the Municipal House.

THE BASICS

- G7
- Náměstí Republiky 5
- 222 002 100
- Check locally
- Náměstí Republiky
- Few

HIGHLIGHTS

- Entrance canopy and mosaic *Homage to Prague*
- Smetanova síň (Smetana Hall), with frescos symbolizing the dramatic arts
- Mayor's Suite, with paintings by Mucha
- Rieger Hall, with Myslbek sculptures
- Palacký Room, with paintings by Preisler

The prosaic name 'Municipal House' fails utterly to convey anything of the character of this extraordinary art nouveau building, a gloriously extravagant early-20th-century confection on which every artist of the day seems to have left his stamp.

City council citadel Glittering like some gigantic, flamboyant jewel, more brightly than ever since its 1997 restoration, the Obecní dům is linked to the blackened Prašná brána (Powder Tower, ▷ 36), last relic of the Old Town's fortifications and long one of the city's main symbols. The intention of the city fathers in the first years of the 20th century was to add an even more powerful element to the cityscape that would celebrate the glory of the Czech nation and Prague's place within it. The site of the old Royal Palace was selected, and no expense was spared to erect a megastructure in which the city's burgeoning life could expand. Begun in 1902, the great edifice was ceremonially opened in 1911.

Ornamental orgy The building schedule included meeting and assembly rooms, cafés, restaurants, bars, even a pâtisserie, while the mayor was provided with particularly luxurious quarters. The 1,149-seat Smetana Hall, home of the Prague Symphony Orchestra, is a temple to the muse of Bohemian music. Everything is encrusted with lavish decoration, in stucco, glass, mosaic, murals, metalwork and textiles.

Staroměstské náměstí

HIGHLIGHTS

- Orloj (Astronomical Clock) from the 15th century
- Council Hall and Clock Tower of Old Town Hall
- Sgraffitoed House at the Minute dated 1611 (No. 2)
- Kostel sv Mikuláše (the baroque Church of St. Nicholas)
- Jan Hus Memorial of 1915
- Palác Kinských (▷ 36)
- The Gothic Dům u Kamenného Zvonu (House at the Stone Bell)
- Arcaded houses Nos. 22–26, with baroque façades and medieval interiors and cellars

TIP

- Climb the tower of the Old Town Hall for one of the best views over Prague's red-tiled roofs.

Visitors throng the Old Town Square all year, entertained by street performers, refreshed at outdoor cafés and enchanted by the Astronomical Clock and the cheerful façades of the old buildings.

Martyrs and mournful memories The Old Town Square has not always been so jolly. The marketplace became a scene of execution of Hussites in the 15th century and 27 prominent Protestants were put to death in 1621 (they are commemorated by white crosses in the paving stones). In 1945, in a final act of spite, diehard Nazis demolished a whole wing of the Old Town Hall; the site has still not been built on.

Striking clock First installed during the 15th century, the Orloj (Astronomical Clock) not only

Clockwise from the left: Old Town Square with Týn Church in the background; detail of a decorated house of 1610; the Astronomical Clock; the square in the sunshine; the painted calendar below the Astronomical Clock; one of the 27 white crosses which are set in the paving stones before the chapel

tells the time, but shows the position of the sun, moon and stars, while its lower dial shows the signs of the Zodiac and the changes of the seasons. Its hourly procession of carved figures is one of the city's great spectacles.

Around the square The hub of the square is the Jan Hus Memorial, an extraordinary art nouveau sculpture whose base is one of the few places in the square where you can sit without having to buy a drink. To your left rise the blackened towers of the Týn Church (▷ 36), while to your right is the Old Town Hall, an attractively varied assembly of buildings and, a bit farther, the city's second St. Nicholas's Church. The fine town houses surrounding the square are a study in various architectural styles from Gothic to Gothic Revival.

THE BASICS

- F/G7
- Staroměstské náměstí
- Restaurants and cafés
- Staroměstská
- Fair

Uměleckoprůmyslové muzeum

The exterior of the museum (middle); stained glass (left); an exhibit (below)

THE BASICS

www.upm.cz
F6
17 listopadu 2
251 093 111 Tue 10–8, Wed–Sun 10–6
Café (Mon–Fri 10–6; Sat, Sun 10.30–6)
Staroměstská
Few
Moderate

HIGHLIGHTS

- Pietra dura scene of a town by Castnicci
- Beer glasses engraved with card players
- Boulle commode and cabinet
- Monumental baroque furniture by Dientzenhofer and Santini
- Meissen Turk on a rhino
- Holic porcelain figures
- Harrachov glass
- Klášterec figurines of Prague characters
- Biedermeier cradle
- Surprise view down into the Old Jewish Cemetery

The pompous façade of Prague's Decorative Arts Museum merely hints at the riches within. A steep flight of stairs leads visitors to treasure chambers full of fine furniture, glass, porcelain, clocks and more.

Riverside reclaimed Looking something like a miniature Louvre, the Decorative Arts Museum was built in 1901 in an area that, by the end of the 19th century, had turned its back on the river and become a jumble of storage depots and timber yards. The city leaders decided to beautify it with fine public buildings and riverside promenades. The School of Arts and Crafts (1884) and the Rudolfinum concert hall and gallery (1890) preceded the museum; the University's Philosophy Building (1929), which completed the enclosure of what is now Jan Palach Square, followed it.

Decorative delights The museum's collections are incredibly rich and diverse, numbering nearly 200,000 objects from all over the world, but with special emphasis on the glorious craft heritage of the Czech lands. Carefully chosen items are arranged in a series of imaginative themed displays such as 'Story of the Fribe' (covering textiles of all kinds), 'Born in Fire' (glass and porcelain) and 'Print and Image' (books, graphics and photography). While there are objects from every era, the contribution on the art nouveau and art deco movements are particularly decorative.

More to See

BETLÉMSKÁ KAPLE (BETHLEHEM CHAPEL)

You must see this barnlike structure where Jan Hus preached to really appreciate the deeply nonconformist traditions so thoroughly obscured by centuries of imposed Catholicism. The chapel, in the Old Town, was totally reconstructed in the 1950s.

F7 Betlémské náměstí Apr–Oct Tue–Sun 10–6.30; rest of year 10–5.30 Restaurants and cafés nearby Národní třída Inexpensive

DŮM U ČERNÉ MATKY BOŽÍ (HOUSE AT THE BLACK MADONNA)

This striking example of Czech Cubist architecture, designed by Josef Gočár (1912), stands squarely at the corner of Celetná Street in the heart of the Old Town. It houses a fine collection of Czech Cubism.

G7 Ovocný trh 19 224 211 746 Daily Tue–Sun 10–6 Náměstí Republiky Moderate

DŮM U ZLATÉHO PRSTENU (HOUSE AT THE GOLDEN RING)

The Prague City Gallery's fine collection of 20th- and 21st-century Czech art is housed here. The gallery stages large exhibitions a few steps away at the House at the Stone Bell, a Gothic tower house that restorers discovered behind a rococo façade in the 1960s.

G7 Týnská 6 224 827 022 Tue–Sun 10–6 Cafés and restaurants Staroměstská Moderate

KLEMENTINUM

Now the home of the National Library, this vast complex arranged around a sequence of courtyards was begun by the Jesuits in the late 16th century. A guided tour takes in some of the sumptuous interiors, but only concertgoers get to see the gorgeous Mirror Chapel.

F7 Klementinum 221 663 111/603 231 241 Core hours: daily 2–6 Cafés and restaurants Staroměstská Moderate

The Black Madonna House is a Cubist style building which houses the museum of Czech Cubism

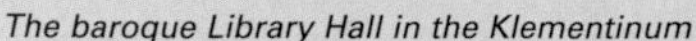

The baroque Library Hall in the Klementinum

KOSTEL PANNY MARIE PŘED TÝNEM (TÝN CHURCH)

Among the city's best-known landmarks is this Gothic church, whose twin towers stick up spikily behind the houses of Old Town Square. Inside are some fascinating tombs.
G7 ✉ Týnská and Celetná ⏲ May be open only just before and during services 🍴 Cafés and restaurants nearby Ⓜ Staroměstská or Náměstí Republiky

MUZEUM BEDŘICHA SMETANY (SMETANA MUSEUM)

The museum dedicated to the composer of 'Vltava' is appropriately in a building that rises out of the river.
E7 ✉ Novotného lávka 1 ☎ 222 220 082 ⏲ Wed–Mon 10–noon, 1–5 Ⓜ Staroměstská Inexpensive

PALÁC KINSKÝCH (KINSKY PALACE)

Franz Kafka's family lived and worked in this lovely rococo palace, and in February 1948 the Communist coup d'etat was proclaimed from its balcony. It's part of the National Gallery, with fine Czech landscape paintings.
G7 ✉ Staroměstské náměstí ☎ 224 810 758 ⏲ Tue–Sun 10–6 Ⓜ Staroměstská Moderate

PRAŠNÁ BRÁNA (POWDER TOWER)

This famous gateway, with its chisel roof, was built as a ceremonial entrance to the Old Town. The climb to the top is worthwhile for the views. The tower houses an exhibition devoted to 'Prague Spires'.
G7 ✉ Celetná ⏲ Apr–early Nov daily 10–6 Ⓜ Náměstí Republiky 🚋 Trams 5, 14 to Náměstí Republiky Inexpensive

STAVOVSKÉ DIVADLO (ESTATES THEATRE)

The venue that saw the premiere of Mozart's Don Giovanni in 1787 is a marvel of pristine neoclassical glory. Performances of Wolfgang's greatest hits can be enjoyed here.
G7 ✉ Ovocný trh ☎ 224 901 448 Ⓜ Můstek

Powder Gate Tower (Prašná Brána)

The Estates Theatre, Stavovské divadlo

Staré Město

Explore the crooked streets and squares of the Old Town on a walk that dips in and out of the Royal Way.

DISTANCE: 1.8km (1.2miles) **ALLOW:** 1 hour

START

OBNECÍ DŮM
G7 Náměstí Republiky

❶ From the Municipal House, go along Celetná, then turn right into the courtyard of No.17. This leads you into Štupartská, then into Malá Štupartská to the baroque façade of St James's church.

❷ Go back a few steps, turning right under the archway into Týn Court. Leave by the far entrance and go along the side of the Týn church into Old Town Square.

❸ Leaving the Town Hall on your right, continue into Malé náměstí (Little Square). Turn right, then left into Mariánské náměstí (Marian Square).

❹ Go left out of the square along Husová, passing on the left the Clam-Gallas palace with its muscular atlantes.

❺ Plunge through the crowds thronging the Royal Way and continue a short distance along Husová, turning right into narrow Řetězová.

❻ Continue in the same direction along Anenská, turning left into Anenské náměstí (Agnes Square). The square houses the Theatre at the Balustrade, where Václav Havel began his theatrical career.

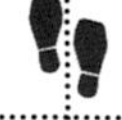

❼ Cross the square into the alleyway leading to Náprstkova; turn right. At the end of the street, go up the steps facing you on the landward side. Use the crossing to the left to cross the busy road to the riverside.

❽ Walk along the river towards Charles Bridge, turning left along the pier. End your walk at Smetana's statue.

END

NOVOTNÉHO LÁVKA
E7 Staroměstská

Shopping

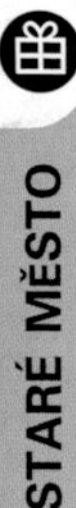

AGHARTA
Jazz, jazz and more jazz on sale at this popular nightspot.
F7 Železná 16 222 211 275 Evenings only Muzeum

ALMA ANTIQUE
Rambling, old-fashioned ground floor and basement establishment with every conceivable kind of antique object.
F7 Valentinská 7 224 813 991 Staroměstská

ANAGRAM
Fiction, philosophy, religion and history in English are the specialties of this bookshop located in the bustling Týn Courtyard.
G7 Týn 4 (between Týnská and Štupartská) 224 895 737 Náměstí Republiky

ANTIKVARIÁT PAŘÍŽSKÁ
One of the few shops on this prestigious boulevard not to deal in designer labels, with walls papered with antique maps and prints.
F7 Pařížská 8 222 321 442 Staroměstská

ART DECO
Glass, ceramics, clothing, jewellery and more from the 1920s and '30s.
F7 Michalská 21 224 223 076 Národní třída

BIG BEN BOOKSHOP
Guidebooks and Czech literature in translation are in good supply at this small, characterful shop.
G7 Malá Štupartská 5 224 826 565 Náměstí Republiky

BOTANICUS
Organic products—soap, cosmetics, teas, herbs and spices—produced on a farm in Lysá nad Labem under the expert supervision of a British specialist. Botanics has several other outlets, including one in the Týn Courtyard.
F7 Michalská 2 224 212 977 Můstek

CELETNÁ CRYSTAL
Sells good-quality Bohemian glass.
G7 Celetná 15 224 811 376 Náměstí Republiky

REPRODUCTIONS
Genuine art nouveau objects can be expensive, Cubist artefacts astronomically so. Superb, though far from cheap reproductions of the latter can be found in an appropriate setting on the ground floor of the Cubist Dům U Černé Matky Boží (Black Madonna House) at the eastern end of Celetná Ovocný trh 19.

CLASSIC MODEL
Miniature trains galore, even a tiny model of a classic 1960s red-and-cream Prague train.
F8 Bartolomějská 3 224 228 101 Národní třída

COUNTRY LIFE
Healthy natural foods—elsewhere hard to find in this calorie-addicted city.
F7 Melantrichova 15 Můstek

CULINARIA
Well-stocked international delicatessen. A particular boon for those more enthusiastic about the culinary products of the Mediterranean lands than those of Central Europe.
F8 Skořepka 9 224 247 237 Národní třída/Můstek

DOROTHEUM
This branch of the long-established Vienna auction house has a fine range of antiques of all kinds. No bargains, but no rip-offs either.
G7 Ovocný trh 2 224 222 001 Můstek or Náměstí Republiky

DŮM VÍN ČESKÉ REPUBLIKY
The 'Winehouse of the Czech Republic' offers (for a fee) tastings from its huge range of Bohemian and Moravian vintages.
G7 Týn 637/7

☎ 224 827 155 Ⓜ Náměstí Republiky

GALERIE PEITHNER-LICHTENFELS

Modern Czech and Austrian art, including works from the period between the wars. The wide range of paintings, prints and sculptures makes a purchase possible for every pocket.
✚ F7 ✉ Michalská 12 ☎ 224 227 680 Ⓜ Můstek

GRANÁT

Bohemian garnets are world-famous; this factory shop has the most varied selection.
✚ G6 ✉ Dlouhá 30 ☎ 222 315 612 Ⓜ Náměstí Republiky

HAVELSKÁ/V KOTCÍCH

Atmospheric market for fruits, vegetables and souvenirs.
✚ F7 ✉ Staré Město ⏲ Daily Ⓜ Můstek

HYNEK CIBULKA UZENÁŘSTVÍ

Locals throng this classy butcher's shop, which features a bewildering array of Central European sausages.
✚ F8 ✉ Uhelný trh 8 ☎ 224 215 253 Ⓜ Můstek

IVANA FOLLOVÁ ART & FASHION

A large shop in the Týn courtyard offering high-quality, locally made silk dresses and scarves, jewellery and ceramics.
✚ G7 ✉ Týn 1 (between Týnská and Štupartská) ☎ 224 895 460 Ⓜ Náměstí Republiky

KNIHKUPECTVÍ U ČERNÉ MATKY BOŽÍ

A large, well-stocked bookshop that carries a good selection of coffee-table books in English. Unmissable location in the Cubist House at the Black Madonna (▷ 38), which means you can retire to the stylish café to peruse your purchases.
✚ G7 ✉ Celetná 34 ☎ 224 211 275 Ⓜ Náměstí Republiky

KOTVA

The Anchor was completed in 1975 to a Scandinavian design and for a while was the city's foremost shopping site, although the range of goods would have seemed basic to Western consumers.
✚ G7 ✉ Náměstí Republiky 8 Ⓜ Náměstí Republiky

MUSIC MISCELLANY

In addition to excellent CDs of music by the classical composers most closely associated with the city (Mozart, Dvořák, Smetana...), Prague shops stock highly individual pop music (Šum Svistu, or Laura and her Tigers, Psi vojáci...). Even more distinctive are the brass bands—the best you've ever heard—pumping out Czech (yes, Czech) old-time preferences such as 'Roll Out the Barrel' (Škoda lásky).

LISKA

Like other Central Europeans, Czechs wear their furs freely and without shame. This opulent establishment is a branch of the famous Austrian dealer in fine furs.
✚ G7 ✉ Železná 1 ☎ 224 221 928 Ⓜ Můstek

MANUFAKTURA

Natural goods and traditional handicrafts, including linens, blankets, hand-dyed fabrics, wooden toys and Christmas ornaments.
✚ F7 ✉ Melantrichova 17 ☎ 221 632 411 Ⓜ Můstek

TUPESY

Charming folk ceramics from Moravia, sold to the sound of *cembalorn* music from that region.
✚ F7 ✉ Havelská 21 ☎ 224 214 176 Ⓜ Můstek

Entertainment and Nightlife

AGHARTA JAZZ CENTRUM

Cramped but enjoyable for local and international jazz, with cocktails and snacks. CD shop.
F7 Železná 16
222 211 275 Muzeum

DIVADLO IMAGE (IMAGE THEATRE)

Visitor-oriented theatre with black light shows, featuring dance, mime and music.
F7 Pařížská 4 222 314 448 Staroměstská

JAZZ CLUB U STARÉ PANÍ

Some of the best local musicians play in this central jazz club.
F7 Michalská 9
224 228 090 Můstek

KLEMENTINUM

This vast complex (▷ 35) hosts chamber concerts in its Hall of Mirrors (Zrcadlová síň).
F7 Entrances at Karlova 1, Mariánské náměsti and Křižovnické náměstí
Staroměstská

NÁRODNÍ DIVADLO MARIONET (NATIONAL MARIONETTE THEATRE)

Adaptations of operas are among the attractions. There are matinees for youngsters.
F7 Žatecká 1 224 819 322–24 Můstek

ROXY

Unusual underground establishment that has DJs and live acts of every conceivable stripe, including stars of world music.
G6 Dlouhá 33
224 826 296 Náměstí Republiky

RUDOLFINUM

The Dvořák Hall of this splendid neo-Renaissance hall on the Vltava is the home of the Czech Philharmonic Orchestra. The Little (or Suk) Hall is used for chamber concerts.
F6 Náměstí Jana Palacha 227 059 352
Staroměstská

SMETANOVA SÍŇ (SMETANA HALL)

www.fok.cz
Part of the sumptuously decorated Municipal House (▷ 30), and home of the Prague Symphony Orchestra.
G7 Náměstí Republiky 5 222 002 336
Náměstí Republiky

CINEMA

Prague has dozens of cinemas. Many of the older establishments are around Wenceslas Square, while multiplexes tend to be linked to the shopping malls that have sprung up in the suburbs. Only a couple of Metro stops from downtown, the largest of these is Palace Cinemas in the Nový Smíchov mall. Most English-language films are shown in the original version, with subtitles in Czech.

STAVOVSKÉ DIVADLO (ESTATES THEATRE)

The spectacular auditorium of this theatre, with five tiers of box seats, is a wonderful setting for opera. Performances are at 7.30pm with matinees on weekends. Also ▷ 36.
G7 Ovocný trh
224 901 448 Můstek

TA FANTASTIKA

Another spectacle based on the black light fusion of dance, mime and music—a spin-off from the hugely successful Laterna Magika. The stage also hosts pop musicals starring local idols.
F7 Karlova 8 222 221 366 Staroměstská

UNGELT JAZZ 'N' BLUES CLUB

More pub than club, this newish place concentrates on local talent.
G7 Týn 2 (enter from Týnská ulička) 224 895 748 Můstek or Staroměstská

VAGON

All-night, every night, rock or reggae in this dive on the Old Town side of Národní třída.
F8 Národní třída 25
221 085 599
Národní třída

Restaurants

PRICES

Prices are approximate, based on a 3-course meal for one person.

£££	over £800Kč
££	400Kč–£800Kč
£	under 400Kč

ALLEGRO (£££)

The riverside restaurant of the prestigious Four Seasons Hotel has been voted the country's best for its Bohemian specialties and cosmopolitan cuisine.
F7 Veleslavínova 2a
221 427 000
Staroměstská

AMICI MIEI (£££)

Italian film posters, elegant décor and sublime food.
G6 Vězeňská 5
224 816 688
Staroměstská

AU GOURMAND CAFÉ (£)

Freshly baked sweet and savoury treats in a beautifully restored art nouveau butcher's shop.
G7 Dlouhá 10
222 312 694
Staroměstská

BAROCK (££)

Trendy bar-restaurant well located on Prague's glitziest shopping street.
F6 Pařížská 24
222 329 221
Staroměstská

CHEZ MARCEL (£–££)

This comfy café/restaurant serves up typical bistro fare. Popular among expats.
G6 Haštalská 12
222 315 676 Tram 5, 8, 14 to Dlouhá třída

COUNTRY LIFE (£)

Healthy eating and food shopping in the heart of the Old Town.
F7 Melantrichova 15
224 213 366 Můstek

KING SOLOMON (£££)

Good kosher food and a lovely winter garden.
F7 Široka 8, Josefov
224 818 752
Staroměstská

KLUB ARCHITEKTŮ (£–££)

This romanesque cellar next to the Bethlehem chapel has vegetarian options, along with Czech staples served with a twist. English menus also available.
F8 Betlémské náměstí 5a 224 401 214
Národní třída

TURKISH COFFEE

Espresso, cappuccino and most other coffees can now be found in Prague, but don't be surprised if you get served a traditional 'turecká káva'. This is Czech-style Turkish coffee—that is, hot water poured right over ground coffee. Invariably served in a piping-hot glass with no handle. Be sure to stop swallowing—that is before you disturb the deposit of coffee grounds at the bottom of the cup.

KOLKOVNA (£–££)

This updated take on the traditional pub, near Old Town Square, serves Czech staples along with pastas and salads. Great for groups, but be sure to reserve in advance.
F6 V Kolkovně 8o
224 819 701
Staroměstská

ORANGE MOON (££)

See for yourself how well Czech beer complements Thai, Burmese and Indian cuisine.
G6 Rámová 5 222 325 119 Staroměstská

PLZEŇSKÁ RESTAURACE (££)

In the basement of the Municipal House (▷ 30–31) is this art nouveau designer's idea of what a Bohemian beer hall should look like. The food is standard pub fare such as goulash.
G7 Náměstí Republiky 5 222 002 780
Náměstí Republiky

POTREFENÁ HUSA (£)

This is one of several branches of the 'Shot

Goose', bright, cheerful and very contemporary bars with a useful line in satisfying Czech and international food.
F6 Bílkova 5 222 326 626 Staroměstská

RED HOT & BLUES (£–££)
Cajun chicken, creole gumbo and other southern specialties, plus live jazz and blues in the evenings.
G7 Jakubská 12 222 314 639 Náměstí Republiky

RYBÍ TRH (£££)
Sumptuous fish restaurant in the enchanting Týn Court.
G7 Týn 5 224 895 449 Staroměstská, Náměstí Republiky

SLAVIA (£)
This classic Central European café, once the haunt of dissident intellectuals, has a superb view over the Vltava.
E8 Smetanovo nábřeží 2 224 218 493 Národní třída

STOLETÍ (£)
When was the last time stuffed avocado made you think of Greta Garbo? Or baked turkey breast Harry Truman? At this quirky place, the dishes are all named after the famous. Czech with a twist.
F8 Karoliny Světlé, 222 220 008 Národní třída

U MEDVÍDKŮ (£)
Budvar, from the town of České Budějovice in southern Bohemia, is probably the best-known Bohemian beer apart from Pilsener. Try it on tap, in the garden, in summer.
F8 Na Perštýně 7 224 220 930 Národní třída

VEGGIE REVOLUTION

Before 1989, vegetarians venturing to Prague were liable to be served endless omelettes, perhaps with extra dumplings. Czechs still like their rich and hearty meat-based dishes, but waiters and others are no longer fazed when a foreigner expresses an interest in something else.

U MODRÉ KACHNIČKY II (££)
The 'Blue Duckling II' is an offshoot of the original establishment in Malá Strana (▷ 94). Both offer a sophisticated take on traditional Bohemian cuisine, featuring succulent game.
F7 Michalská 16 224 213 418 Můstek

U VEJVODŮ (£)
This old pub has been remodelled, enlarged and cleaned up, and now the Pilsner palace appeals to visitors and locals alike.
F7 Jilská 4 224 219 999 Národní třída

Nové Město

Prague's commercial heart beats strongly in the New Town. The district is focused on a series of squares; foremost is the Václavské náměstí, with Národní muzeum and the statue of Good King Wenceslas.

6
7
8
9
10
11
12
C
D
E
F
Karlovy lázně
Náprstkova
Náprstkovo muzeum
Betlémská
Konviktská
Bartolomějská
Karoliny Světlé
Na Perštýně
Národní třída
Vltava
Smetanovo nábřeží
Divadelní
Krocínova
Viola
Národní divadlo
most Legií
Střelecký ostrov
Národní
sv Voršil
Voršilská
Mikulandská
Reduta
Laterna magika
Ostrovní
V Jirchářích
Žofín
Masarykovo nábřeží
Na Struze
Pštrossova
Opatovická
Černá
Slovanský ostrov
Vojtěšská
sv Vojtěch
Muzeum Pivo
Křemencova
Myslíkova
Odboru
Mánes
Na Zderaze
Svatého Cyril a Metoděj
Jiráskovo nám
Jiráskovo náměstí
Dittrichova
JIRÁSKŮV MOST
RESSLOVA
Tančící dům
ČVUT
Václavská
Gorazdova
Trojanova
Moráň
Palackého náměstí
Na Moráni
Palackého most
Palackého nám
sv Jan na skalce
klášter Na Slovanech (Emauzy)
Vyšehradská
Dřevná
RAŠÍNOVO NÁBŘEŽÍ
Podskalská
Trojická
Nejsv Trojice
Ladova
Slovany
Plavecká
Na výtoni
Na hrobci
Výtoň
SVOBODOVA
Libušina
Vratislavova
sv Petra Pavel Vyšehrad
Vyšehradské sady
Ústav pro péči o matku a dítě
0
250 m
0
250 yds

Vltava
ŠTEFÁNIKŮV MOST
LUDVIKA SVOBODY
TĚŠNOVSKÝ TUNEL
min dopravy
min zem
Na Františku
Minist prům a obchodu
Poštovní muzeum
Lannova
HOLBOVA
KLIMENTSKÁ
Hradební
Revoluční
Klimentská
Barvířská
Samcova
Mlynářská
Helmova
Půtova
Těšnov
WILSONOVA
KE ŠTVANICI
Soukenická
Petrská
Biskupská
Bílá labuť
Florenc
Sokolovská
Muzeum hlavního města Prahy
KŘIŽÍKOVA
Hudební divadlo
Truhlářská
Zlatnická
Na poříčí
Masarykovo nádraží
V celnici
Náměstí Republiky
ŽEL ST MASARYKOVO NÁDRAŽÍ
Hybernská
HUSITSKÁ
Seifertova
Senovážná
Slovanský dům
Hlavní nádraží
U Bulhara
Bolzanova
Na Příkopě
Nekázanka
Senovážné náměstí
Jindřišská
Muchovo muzeum
sv Jindřich
Panská
Jeruzalémská
Opletalova
Vrchlického sady
Muzeum komunismu
U půjčovny
Růžová
Panny Marie sněžné
Můstek
Bredov palác
HLAVNÍ NÁDRAŽÍ
Václavské
Olivova
Daňkův palác
Františkánská zahrada
div Adria
Václavské náměstí
Politických vězňů
Petschk palác
Washingtonova
WILSONOVA
Státní opera
Vodičkova
Rokoko
div ABC
Palackého
Jungmannova
Vladislavova
V jámě
Štěpánská
Ve Smečkách
div Kalich
Muzeum
Radio Svob Evropa
LEGEROVA
sv Václav
Vodičkova
Obvodní úřad
Navrátilova
Div-Blanik
Krakovská
MEZIBRANSKÁ
Národní muzeum
Vinohradská
Čelakovského sady
Škólská
V Řeznické
Řeznická
Rubešova
Římská
ŽITNÁ
Malá
Na Rybníčku
V tůních
Hálková
SOKOLSKÁ
ANGLICKÁ
Mikovcova
IP Pavlova
Vocelova
Bělehradská
sv Štěpán
JEČNÁ
náměstí I P Pavlova
Jugoslávská
Štěpánská
sv Ignác
Salmovská
I P Pavlova
NOVÉ MĚSTO
Lipová
Kateřinská
Muzeum A Dvořáká
Ke Karlovu
Na bojišti
RUMUNSKÁ
svatá Kateřina
Všeobecná Fakultuí nemocnice
Viničná
Tyršova
psychiat klinika
Fügnerovo nám
LEGEROVA
Apolinářská
Botanická zahrada univerzity Karlovy
Zemská porodnice
sv Apolinář
Wenzigova
univerzity Karlovy
Studničkova
Albertov
B Němcové
P Marie
Muzeum policie ČR
Horská
Albertov
Hlavova
Votočkova
NA SLUPI
Folimanka
Botič
SEKANINOVA
NUSELSKÝ MOST
Ostrčilovo náměstí
Oldřichova
Nezamyslova
Svatoplukova
JAROMÍROVA
P Maria
sv Martina
SLAVOJOVA
Lumírova
V pevnosti
Krokova
Jedličkův ústav
G
H
J

Muchovo muzeum

Advertising poster (left); detail of a window sculpture (below)

THE BASICS

www.mucha.cz
G7
Kaunický palác, Panská 7
224 216 415
Daily 10–6
Moderate
Můstek or Náměstí Republiky
Tram 3, 9, 14, 24 to Jindřišská

HIGHLIGHTS

- Sarah Bernhardt Gismonda poster
- Moravian Teachers' Choir poster
- Re-created Paris studio
- Biographical film

Best known for his posters of languorous Parisian lovelies advertising everything from champagne to cigarettes, art nouveau artist Alfons Mucha was a proud Czech patriot whose later work celebrated his country's independence.

From Alphonse to Alfons Alfons Mucha (1860–1939) was an émigré Czech who first found fame in Paris when he created a sensation with a stunning poster of the actress Sarah Bernhardt. Mucha was an idealist who hoped that art nouveau would break down the barriers between high art and everyday design. After his return to Prague, he worked on a variety of projects, from decorating the interiors of the Obecní dům (▷ 30) to designing stamps and banknotes for the new Czechoslovak Republic and stained glass for St. Vitus's Cathedral.

Museum exhibits Housed in the 18th-century Kaunic Palace, this museum shows off Mucha memorabilia, as well as drawings, paintings and sculpture, and an atmospheric re-creation of the Paris studio he shared with Rodin and Gauguin. In his later years, Mucha devoted himself to a sequence of 20 immense canvases depicting high points in the history of the Czechs and other Slav peoples. The paintings were intended to be put on permanent display in the capital, and although a Prague home is planned, they continue to languish in a provincial castle. The museum here shows an excellent English-language film about them.

Exterior views of the theatre, one reflected in a modern building (below)

Národní divadlo

Even if the thought of a classical play performed in Czech doesn't enthrall you, don't miss the National Theatre. It is, perhaps, the greatest of Prague's collective works of art, decorated by the finest artists of the age.

National drama Theatre in Prague still spoke with a German voice in the mid-19th century. Money to build a specifically Czech theatre was collected from 1849 onward, without support from German-dominated officialdom. The foundation stone was laid in 1868 with much festivity, then in 1881, just before the first performance, the theatre burned down. Undiscouraged, the populace rallied, and by 1883 it had been completely rebuilt. The opening was celebrated with a grand gala performance of the opera *Libuše* by Smetana, a passionate supporter of the theatre project.

Expanded ambition The National Theatre stands at the New Town end of Most Legií (Legions Bridge), its bulk carefully angled to fit into the streetscape and not diminish the view to Petřín Hill on the far bank. It was given a long-deserved restoration in time for its centenary, and when it reopened in 1983 it had gained a piazza and three annexes, whose architecture has been much maligned, the least unkind comment being that the buildings seem to be clad in bubble-wrap. Prague's popular multimedia show Laterna Magika (▷ 59) performs in one of the buildings, the Nová scéna.

THE BASICS

www.narodni-divadlo.cz
E8
Národní 2
224 901 448
Bar
Tram 6, 9, 18, 21, 22, 23 to Národní divadlo
Few
Opera tickets: inexpensive–moderate

HIGHLIGHTS

- Bronze troikas above the entrance loggia
- Star-patterned roof of the dome
- Frescos in the foyer by Mikoláš Aleš
- Painted ceiling of the auditorium, by František Ženíšek
- Painted stage curtain by Vojtěch Hynais
- View of the theatre from Střelecký Island
- Any performance of an opera from the Czech repertoire

Národní muzeum

The spacious three-floor staircase; sculpture outside the museum

THE BASICS

www.nm.cz
H9
Václavské náměstí 68
224 497 111
Oct–Apr daily 9–5; rest of year daily 10–6. Closed first Tue of month
Café
Muzeum
Few
Moderate; free first Mon of month

HIGHLIGHTS

- Allegorical sculptures on the terrace
- The Pantheon and dome
- Coin collection
- Collection of precious stones
- Skeleton of a whale

Some people find Prague's National Museum disappointing. However, try to enjoy it as a period piece in its own right, for its dusty showcases are as venerable as the building itself.

Top building With its gilded dome crowning the rise at the top of Václavské náměstí (Wenceslas Square, ▷ 50), Prague's National Museum provides a grand finale to the capital's most important street. The neo-Renaissance building was completed in 1891, and at the time was as much an object of pride to the Czech populace as the Národní divadlo (National Theatre, ▷ 47). Such is its presence that some visitors have mistaken it for the parliament building, as did the Soviet gunner who raked its façade with machine-gun fire in August 1968.

An array of -ologies Even if you are not a keen entomologist, paleontologist, zoologist, mineralogist or numismatist, you won't fail to be impressed by the evidence here of the 19th century's great passion for collecting and classifying. Efforts are under way to make the treasures here more accessible and entertaining; there are interactive displays, a schedule of often fascinating temporary exhibits, and a dinosaur display to engage the young. But above all, the building itself is impressive, with its grand stairways, statuary, mosaics and patterned floors. Unlike most attractions in Prague, it's open on Mondays.

St. Martin's Rotunda (below); the river and Vyšehrad (right)

TOP 25

Vyšehrad

Rising high above the River Vltava is Vyšehrad ('High Castle'), where the soothsaying Princess Libuše foresaw the founding of Prague, and where she married her ploughman swain, Přemysl.

Romantic rock Beneath Vyšehrad's 19th-century neo-Gothic Church of St. Peter and St. Paul are the remains of a far earlier, Romanesque church that once served the royal court. But it was in the 19th century, with the rise of Romantic ideas about history and nationhood, that poets, playwrights and painters celebrated the great fortress-rock, elaborating the story of Libuše. Most of their efforts have been forgotten, though Smetana's 'Vyšehrad', part of his glorious tone-poem *Má Vlast*, remains popular. The nation's great and good have been buried in the National Cemetery (or Pantheon) at Vyšehrad since the late 19th century. Smetana himself is here, and fellow composer Dvořák. On the lawns nearby are freestanding sculptures of Libuše and other legendary figures by Josef Václav Myslbek, the creator of Wenceslas in Wenceslas Square.

Vltava views Everyone driving along the main riverside highway has to pay homage to Vyšehrad, as the road and tram tracks twist and turn and then tunnel through the high rock protruding into the Vltava. In the 1920s the whole hilltop was turned into a public park, with wonderful views up and down the river (▷ 52).

THE BASICS

www.praha-vysehrad.cz
F12
Information centre: V Pevnosti, Vyšehrad. Brick Gate: Vratislavova, Vyšehrad
Prague Fortifications Museum: Apr–Octdaily 9.30–6; rest of year daily 9.30–5. Cemetery: Apr–Oct daily 8–7; rest of year daily 8–5
Restaurant
Vyšehrad
Trams 3, 16, 17, 21 to Výtoň then a steep uphill walk
Fair
Park and cemetery: free
Museum: inexpensive

HIGHLIGHTS

- National Cemetery graves and memorials and the Slavín mausoleum
- St. Martin's Rotunda (Romanesque church)
- Cihelná brána (Brick Gate), with Prague Fortifications Museum
- Ramparts walk
- Neo-Gothic Kostel sv Petra a Pavla (Church of St. Peter and St. Paul)

Václavské náměstí

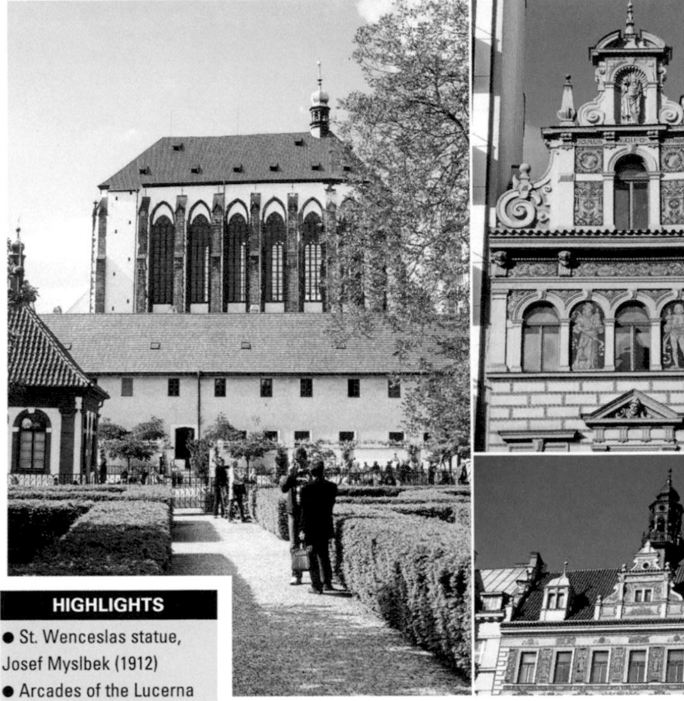

HIGHLIGHTS

- St. Wenceslas statue, Josef Myslbek (1912)
- Arcades of the Lucerna Palace
- Hotel Evropa, completed 1905 (No. 25)
- 1920s Functionalist Bat`a and Lindt buildings (Nos. 4, 6)
- Ambassador, late art nouveau hotel of 1912 (No. 5)
- Memorial to Jan Palach
- 1950s Soviet-style Jalta Hotel (No. 45)
- Former Bank of Moravia of 1916 (Nos. 38–40)
- Art nouveau Peterka building of 1900 (No. 12)
- Koruna Palace of 1914 (No. 1)

Despite its sometimes rather seedy air, Wenceslas Square is still the place where the city's heart beats most strongly, and to meet someone 'beneath the horse' (the Wenceslas statue) remains a thrill.

When is a square not a square? When it's a boulevard. 'Václavák', 700m (763 yards) long, slopes gently up to the imposing façade of the National Museum (▷ 48). Just down the slope stands the statue of 'Good King' Wenceslas on his sprightly steed, a good place for a rendezvous at any time of day and night.

History in the making Many dramas of modern times have been played out in Wenceslas Square. The new state of Czechoslovakia was proclaimed here in 1918, and in 1939 German

Clockwise from left: Frantiskanska zahrada or Franciscan Garden, reached via the arcades of the Palac Alfa; sgraffito façade on a building; advertisement on top of building on the corner of Vodickova and Vaclavské náměstí; classical statues support a bay window on No. 8 Vaclavské náměstí; Wiehluv dům (exterior views)

tanks underlined the republic's demise. In 1968, more tanks arrived—this time to crush the Prague Spring of Alexander Dubček. To protest at the Soviet occupation, Jan Palach burned himself to death here in 1969, and in 1989 Dubček and Václav Havel waved from the balcony of No. 36 as Czechs crowded here to celebrate the collapse of Communism.

Museum of modern architecture The procession of buildings lining both sides of the square, from the resplendent art nouveau Hotel Evropa to the elegant Functionalist Bat'a Store, tells the story of the Czech contribution to 20th-century architecture and design. More intriguing are the arcades that burrow deep into the buildings, creating a labyrinth of boutiques, theatres, cafés and cinemas.

THE BASICS

- G–H8
- Václavské náměstí
- Many restaurants and cafés
- Můstek or Muzeum
- Fair

TIP

- People-watching on the square can be accomplished from the terrace cafés on the east side, which catch the midday and afternoon sun.

Vltava Boat Trip

HIGHLIGHTS

- Frank Gehry's 'Dancing Building'
- Charles Bridge from beneath
- Art nouveau Čech Bridge

TIP

- It's worth choosing a fine day and sitting on the open deck but you will be exposed to the sun—so don't forget to wear sunscreen.

A cruise is a wonderful way to see Prague from a different angle. Some of the bridges are works of art, and there are many other fascinating river sights immortalized by Bedřich Smetana.

National river The Vltava (sometimes known by its German name of Moldau) rises high in the hills along the Austrian border. Flowing north into the Elbe (Labe in Czech) some 40km (25 miles) downstream from Prague, its waters eventually discharge into the North Sea. Mostly tranquil, the river's mood can change suddenly; its banks have often burst, and in 1890 it swept away several of the arches of Charles Bridge. Dams upstream were supposed to have tamed it, but failed to prevent the disastrous flood of August 2002, when much of

Clockwise from the left: large river boats cruise the Vltava, overlooked by the row of buildings which line Masaryk Embankment; the Vltava; a couple in a small row boat passing a swan; mature trees obscure some of the colour-washed façades of the buildings on the riverbank, with the towers of St. Vitus's Cathedral behind

downtown was inundated. Despite such incidents, it's the most loved of Czech rivers.

Riverside delights Trips head downstream from Rašínovo nábřeží (Rašín Embankment) to Ostrov Štavnice (Štavnice Island), where they turn about and tie up at the landing stage by Čechův most (Čech Bridge). You pass beneath five bridges as well as Charles Bridge, manoeuvre through a lock, and get close-up views of several of the islands. To port there's Dětský ostrov (Children's Island), with its playgrounds, to starboard Slovanský ostrov (Slavonic Island) with the Žofín concert hall, then in the middle of the stream Střelecký ostrov (Shooters' Island), where marksmen used to practise. You also see the weirs over which lumbermen used to pole their great chains of timber rafts.

THE BASICS

Prague Steam Navigation Co.
www.paraplavba.cz
✉ Rašínovo nábřeží
☎ 224 931 013; 224 930 017
🕒 Mid-Mar to early Nov, daily 3.30pm
💰 Moderate
? Until the completion of road improvements, cruises may start from a temporary landing stage upstream

More to See

KARLOVO NÁMĚSTÍ

Karlovo náměstí (Charles Square) is more of a park than a square, and is a useful resting place when pounding the pavements becomes too tiring in this spread-out part of town.

MUZEUM HLAVNÍHO MĚSTA PRAHY (CITY MUSEUM)

This late 19th-century building contains exhibits telling the story of Prague's evolution from the earliest times. The star is a scale model of the city as it was in the 1820s and 1830s. Most of the extensive collections are in storage, but selections are shown in rotation.

J6 Na Poříčí 52, north Nové Město 224 816 773 Tue–Sun 9–6 Florenc Inexpensive

MUZEUM KOMUNISMU

www.museumofcommunism.com

The Museum of Communism is a private venture, which has attracted much controversy. The museum contrasts Communism's Utopian dreams with the grim reality of empty shops, meaningless slogans and pervasive policing. An upbeat note is struck at the end, however, with a short film about the Velvet Revolution, which brought an end to the oppressive regime.

G7 Na Příkopě 10 224 212 966 Daily 9–9 Adult moderate, child free Můstek

MUZEUM POLICIE ČR (POLICE MUSEUM)

This museum recovered quickly from the collapse of the old order in 1989 and gives an upbeat account of Czech policing, with lots of gore and weaponry on show in what was once the Karlov Monastery.

G11 Ke Karlovu 1 224 922 183 Tue–Sun 10–5 I P Pavlova or Vyšehrad Inexpensive

PANNY MARIE SNĚŽÉ

The great Gothic Church of Our Lady of the Snows was intended by Emperor Charles IV to rival St. Vitus's Cathedral and to dominate the skyline of the New Town. But

Novomestska radnice (Town Hall) on Karlovo náměstí

Carved figures inside the Church of Our Lady of the Snows

the Hussite Troubles ended building work, and only the chancel was completed. The best view of the exterior is from the Franciscans' Garden. The interior demonstrates both Gothic mastery of space and baroque determination not to be outdone; the huge black and gold high altar of 1650 reaches into the 30m-high (100ft) medieval vaults.
G8 Jungmannovo náměstí 18 224 490 350 Mon–Sat 9–5.15, Sun 12.30–5.15 (no visiting during Mass) Free Můstek Tram 6, 9, 18, 21, 22, 23 to Národní třída

POŠTOVNÍ MUZEUM

www.cpost.cz

The national collection of stamps and postal memorabilia is housed in a 16th-century building with original painted interiors. The emphasis is on stamps from Czechoslovakia and its successor republics, but there's much else besides.
G6 Nové mlýny 2 222 312 006 Tue–Sun 9–12, 1–5 Inexpensive Tram 5, 8, 14 to Dlouhá třída

SVATÉHO CYRIL A METODĚJ

On 18 June 1942, the Baroque Church of Saints Cyril and Methodius was where the Czechoslovak parachutists who had assassinated Reichsprotektor Heydrich made their last stand. Their hiding place in the crypt betrayed by a former comrade, they valiantly held SS troops at bay with a hail of bullets for several hours. Finally, the fire brigade was ordered to flush them out by pumping in water. Rather than fall into the hands of a merciless enemy, the defenders used their last bullets on themselves. Their heroism, and that of the churchmen who hid them, is commemorated by a plaque outside the church and by displays in the crypt itself.
F9 Resslova 9 224 920 686 May–end Sep Tue–Sun 10–5; Oct–end Apr Tue–Sun 10–4 Inexpensive Karlovo náměstí Tram 3, 4, 6, 7, 10, 14, 16, 17, 18, 21, 22, 23, 24 to Karlovo náměstí

A display in the museum housed in the Vila Amerika (▷ 60)

Exterior of the Statni Opera Praha (Opera House; ▷ 60)

The Old and New

This route takes you along the bustling boulevards laid out along the dividing line between the Old and New Towns.

DISTANCE: 1.75km (just over a mile) **ALLOW:** 45 minutes

START

OBECNÍ DŮM
G7 Náměstí Republiky

❶ Turn right and walk along Na Příkopě. Now one of Prague's main shopping streets, it divides—or links—the Old and New Towns.

❷ Pause to look inside the ornate Živnostenská banka, built in 1896. In contrast on the north side of the street is the sober Komerční banka of 1908.

❸ The point where Na Příkopě joins Wenceslas Square is known as the Golden Cross.

❹ Walk up the right-hand side of Wenceslas Square, and turn right into the arcade leading into the attractively landscaped Franciscans' Garden.

❺ Leave the garden via the far corner into Jungmannovo náměstí.

❻ Go past the statue of Josef Jungmann into Národní třída (National Avenue), laid out like Na Příkopě along the line of the Old Town ramparts.

❼ Continue along the left-hand side of Národní třída. In the arcade of No.16 there's a reminder of the Velvet Revolution, a little memorial commemorating the victims of police brutality.

❽ Národní třída ends at the Národní divadlo (National Theatre). Opposite the theatre is the famous Café Slavia.

END

NÁRODNI DIVADLO
E8 Tram: 6, 9, 17, 18, 21, 22, 23

Shopping

ACADEMIA
Good variety of photography books, travel guides, cookbooks and literature in English.
G8 Václavské náměstí 34 224 223 511 Můstek

ANTIKVARIÁT GALERIE MŮSTEK
This old-established firm in the arcade of the Adria Palace is a typical example of the Prague *antikvariát* (antiquarian bookshop), with not just books but an intriguing selection of maps, prints and ephemera.
G8 Národní třída 40 224 949 587 Můstek/Národní třída

BÍLÁ LABUŤ
The White Swan is a long-established department store on an unfashionable but interesting shopping street east of the Old Town.
H6 Na Poříčí 23 222 320 227 Náměstí Republiky

BONTONLAND KORUNA
This is reputedly the biggest music shop in Central Europe. The pop and rock section is vast, classical hardly less so. And there are DVDs and games galore. It is in the labyrinthine basement of the Koruna Palace at the corner of Wenceslas Square and Na příkopě.
G6/7 Václavské náměstí 1 224 473 080 Můstek

CELLARIUS
In the Lucerna arcade off Wenceslas Square, this well-stocked shop sells wines from around the world as well from the vineyards of Bohemia and Moravia.
G8 Štepánská 61 224 210 979 Můstek

CENTRUM FOTOŠKODA
This place is a paradise for camera buffs, stocking every possible kind of photographic equipment (new and secondhand) as well as books and magazines.
G8 Vodičkova 37 222 929 038 Můstek

MALL MAGIC
The arrival of Western-style malls has transformed the shopping scene in Prague. With their bright and shiny, if not innovative, architecture and interior design and their endless temptations, they are a world away from the *potraviny*, the little corner grocers and mini-markets, where most people used to do their daily shopping, and whose death knell they have probably sounded. Many young Praguers seem to spend most of their leisure hours in these temples of consumerism.

DADDY TOYS
In the Černá Růže arcade, this branch of a provincial firm makes tasteful wooden toys for the discerning toddler and parent.
G7 Na Příkopě 12 221 014 607 Můstek

ELAZAR
The Prague outlet of this venerable maker of fine clothes and accessories in fur and leather is on the ground floor of the Černá Růže arcade.
G7 Na Příkopě12 221 014 330 Můstek

FRUITS DE FRANCE
French Fruits changed the face of food shopping in Prague not long after the Velvet Revolution, and is still the place for classy imported foods.
G8 Jindřišská 9 224 220 304 Můstek

GALERIE PYRAMIDA
Not all Czech glass is for serving wine. This spacious shop displays art glass from some of the best Czech designers. Good small bronzes and other objets d'art are also sold.
F8 Národní 11 224 213 117 Národní třída

THE GLOBE BOOKSTORE AND COFFEEHOUSE
A congenial home-away-from-home for Americans and anyone

hungry for literature in English, as well as light meals, American-style coffee (with a free refill before 6pm) and non-alcoholic cocktails. There are newspapers, magazines and internet access, too.
F9 Pštrossova 6
224 934 203 Národní třída or Karlovo náměstí

HATLE ANTIKVARIÁT
Tucked away in a side-street a short distance from Wenceslas Square, this is another fine if dusty example of the Prague *antikvariát*.
G8 Palackého 9
224 947 727
Můstek/Národní třída

HODINÁŘSTVÍ VÁCLAV MATOUŠ
Beautiful antique clocks and watches.
F8 Mikulandská 10
224 930 172 Národní třída

KIWI
As well as a travel agency, this establishment has a comprehensive range of maps and guides to the Czech Republic and beyond. Hanging in the basement is a fascinating collection of wall maps.
G8 Jungmannova 23
224 948 455 Národní třída

MOSER
A palatial first-floor outlet for the fine crystal and porcelain made in Carlsbad (Karlový Vary), along with porcelain from Meissen and Herend. No bargains, but objects of the highest quality are beautifully displayed here.
G7 Na Příkopě 12
224 211 293 Můstek or Náměstí Republiky

MYSLIVOST
This shop caters to that army of Czechs who love the outdoor life. Unusual weatherproof wear and much else.
G8 Jungmannova 25
224 949 014 Národní třída

PALÁC KNIH LUXOR
There's no reason to dispute the claim of the 'Palace of Books' to be the biggest in the country. Descend to the basement for books in English and other foreign languages. The firm has another sizeable store in the Nový Smíchov mall.
G8 Václavské náměstí 41 221 111 364
Můstek/Muzeum

BARGAINS PERHAPS

Czechs are great readers, and until recently new and second-hand books were very inexpensive, many of them in languages other than Czech. Prices have risen considerably, but there are still bargains to be found. That said, prices for antique books are now well in line with those on the international market.

PRAŽSKÉ STAROŽITNOSTI
Jewellery, porcelain and paintings galore.
F8 Mikulandská 8
224 930 572 Národní třída

TESCO
Rival to Kotva (▷ 39) and once bearing the impeccably proletarian name of 'Máj' (May), this department store is now in British hands. A ride up the escalator gives an excellent view of downtown. The basement supermarket is one of the best and busiest in town.
F8 Národní 26
222 003 111
Národní třída

ZLATÝ KŘÍŽ
Lunch-break crowds throng this establishment (the 'Golden Cross'), no doubt because it has what is probably the widest and tastiest range of *obložené chlebičky* (those little open sandwiches, which are a Czech specialty) in Prague, as well as cakes and drinks. You can stand at the buffet and consume your finds or take them away.
G8 Jungmannovo náměstí 19 222 519 451
Můstek/Národní třída

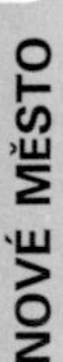

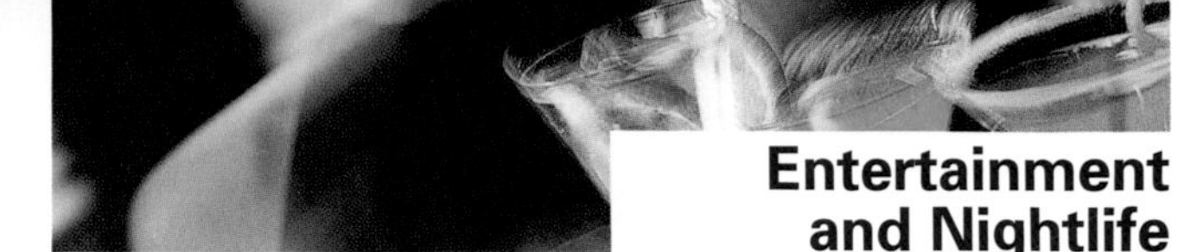

Entertainment and Nightlife

AKKORD

A new club near the Municipal House, featuring everything from funk rock to hard groove jazz.
H7 V Celnici 4
774 101 091 Náměstí Republiky

CASINO PALAIS SAVARIN

Roulette, blackjack, poker, pontoon and 'pokies'.
G7 Na Příkopě 10
224 221 636
Můstek or Náměstí Republiky

ČERNÉ DIVADLO JIŘÍHO SRNEC (JIŘÍ SRNEC BLACK THEATRE)

Legends of magic Prague presented in multimedia format. Jiří Srnec was the originator of black light theatre some 40 years ago.
F8 Divadlo Reduta, Národní třída 20 257 921 835 Národní třída

DIVADLO ARCHA (ARCHA THEATRE)

The Archa Theatre reaches out to non-Czech speakers with a fascinating avant-garde agenda of drama, dance, music and multimedia productions. Tickets for most shows are inexpensive and highly sought after.
H6 Na Poříčí 26
221 716 333
Náměstí Republiky

DIVADLO MINOR (MINOR THEATRE)

This well-known puppetry and drama ensemble puts on a varied schedule designed to appeal to children.
G9 Vodičkova 6
222 231 351 Můstek

DIVADLO PONEC

Contemporary dance theatre with an innovative schedule, based in a building in suburban Žižkov, just outside the New Town.
J7 Husitská 24A
222 721 531 Florenc

HUDEBNÍ DIVADLO KARLÍN

Operettas and musicals are the undemanding fare in this suburban theatre just beyond the inner city. Badly damaged by the 2002 flood, the Karlín Music Theatre is now fully operational again, offering such spectacles as a Czech version of Mel Brooks's *The Producers*.
J6 Křižíkova 10, Karlín 221 868 666
Florenc

ROCK CZECH-STYLE

Before 1989, groups like the Plastic People of the Universe were seen as genuinely subversive of the existing order and were relentlessly hounded by State Security. Nowadays, the rock scene is a confused one, with a lot of fairly mindless imitation of Western trends but plenty of innovation too, featuring fascinating fusions of rock with salsa, klemzer, and other world sounds.

LATERNA MAGIKA

The Magic Lantern's synthesis of film, music, theatre and mime was developed in the 1950s by Alfréd Radok, and continues to intrigue and delight audiences. Some of the most successful shows are reworkings of ancient myths.
F8 Nová scéna of the National Theatre, Národní 4
224 931 482
Národní třída

LUCERNA MUSIC BAR

This is part of the vast complex of the Lucerna Palace, a labyrinth of arcades and passageways that were the work of President Havel's builder-grandfather. Its good-sized ballroom can accommodate visiting groups as well as locals, and although some expats look down on it, it's the place to go for Czech retro.
G8 Vodičkova 36
224 257 108

METROPOLITAN JAZZ CLUB

Swing, ragtime and blues.

G8 Jungmannova 14
224 947 777 Národní třída or Můstek

MILLENNIUM

Glitzy operation in a hotel and retail complex close to the Municipal House.
H7 V Celnici 10
221 033 401 Náměstí Republiky

NÁRODNÍ DIVADLO

The magnificent auditorium of the National Theatre is THE place in which to soak up well-staged performances of such classics from the Czech operatic repertoire as *The Bartered Bride* or *The Cunning Little Vixen*. The schedule also features foreign operas, ballet and drama.
E8 Národní 2 224 901 319, 224 901 448
Národní třída

RADOST FX

One of the most popular spots in town, this club in a street behind the National Museum has been packing them in ever since it was established soon after the Velvet Revolution.
H9 Bělehradská 120
224 254 776 I P Pavlova

REDUTA

Bill Clinton blew his sax at this best-known of Prague jazz locales during his presidential visit to Prague in 1994. Hear dixieland, swing and modern jazz.
F8 Národní 20
224 933 487 Národní třída

ROCK CAFÉ

This downtown café and concert spot is the place to go if you like your rock music hard and very loud.
F8 Národní 20
224 933 947 Národní třída

STÁTNÍ OPERA PRAHA (PRAGUE STATE OPERA)

Originally built in 1888 by Prague's German community as a rival to the exclusively Czech National Theatre, the State Opera has a reputation for more innovative productions of opera, ballet and drama.
H8 Wilsonova 4
224 227 266 Muzeum

VILA AMERIKA

Built as a summer retreat for a rich and cultured Count in the early 18th century, this miniature baroque palace now houses a museum devoted to the composer Antonín Dvořák. There are chamber concerts in its elegant salon, and during the season it makes a lovely setting for an evening show featuring Dvořák's music.
G10 Ke Karlovu 20
224 918 013 I P Pavlova

KEEPING YOU POSTED

Since 1989 there has been a boom in performances of all kinds intended to appeal to foreign visitors. Posters and leaflets will keep you up to date about what's on, as will the English-language Prague Post weekly newspaper.

Restaurants

PRICES

Prices are approximate, based on a 3-course meal for one person.

£££	over £800Kč
££	400Kč–£800Kč
£	under 400Kč

ALCRON (£££)

Hands down, Prague's premier location for seafood. Elegant setting and intimate atmosphere in one of the eating places in the lavishly refurbished hotel of the same name.
G8 Štepánská 40 (in the Radisson SAS Alcron) 222 820 000 Dinner only, closed Sun Muzeum

CAFÉ LOUVRE (£)

A famous establishment now under its original name, the Louvre is decorated in rococo style and offers everything from breakfast to billiards. Also a non-smoking room. Voted café of the year in the columns of the *Prague Post*.
F8 Národní 20 224 930 949 Národní třída

CELNICE (£)

In the splendid old Customs House, this is one of Pilsner Urquell's expertly updated pubs. Reliable Bohemian cuisine at very reasonable prices.
H7 V Celnici 4 224 212 240 Náměstí Republiky

CICALA (£–££)

Authentic Italian, just a block from Wenceslas Square. This is where Italian expats eat out.
G9 Žitná 43 222 210 375

GOVINDA VEGETARIAN CLUB (£)

Plenty of whole food at this Hare Krishna restaurant/bakery/tea room, in a convenient location not far from the art nouveau Obecní dům (Municipal House, ▷ 30–31).
H6 Soukenicka 27 224 816 016 Mon–Fri 11–5 Nám

HOT (££)

On the ground floor of the elegant Jalta Hotel, overlooking the action on Wenceslas Square, this trendy new establishment features imaginative Pacific Rim and other world cuisine.
G8 Václavské náměstí 45 222 247 240 Muzeum/Můstek

CZECH WINES AND SPIRITS

Although little known abroad, Czech wines are surprisingly good, especially both reds and whites from Moravia, and make an interesting souvenir. Spirits are cheap and often excellent. Slivovice (plum brandy) is well known, a supposed cure for all ills, while Becherovka, prepared in Carlsbad to a secret recipe, has a unique and pungent tastes.

HYBERNIA (£)

The latest, and in this case, particularly successful attempt to present decent, inexpensive Czech cuisine to discerning local and international diners. You have a choice of ground floor, courtyard and cellar dining rooms.
H7 Hybernská 7 224 226 004 Náměstí Republiky

KAVÁRNA EVROPA (££)

The art nouveau interior of the café attached to the famous Evropa Hotel is one of the sights of Prague, though service has not always matched the surroundings and at times an entrance fee has been charged.
G8 Václavské náměstí 25 224 215 387

NOVOMĚSTSKÝ PIVOVAR (£)

This brewery serves up its own light and dark lagers along with traditional Czech fare.
G8/9 Vodičkova 20 222 231 662 Also open for breakfast Mon–Fri Tram 3, 9, 14, 24 to Vodičkova

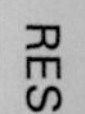

LA PERLE DE PRAGUE (£££)
Atop the controversial 'Fred and Ginger' building, sophisticated, mostly French food, with city and river views.
F9 Rašínovo nábřeží 80 221 984 160 Karlovo náměstí Republiky

POD KŘÍDLEM (£££)
Stylish surroundings and impeccable food. Also close to the National Theatre.
F8 Národní 10 (entrance on Voršilská) 224 933 571 Národní třída

TRITON (££)
Leave the bustle of Wenceslas Square behind as you descend into the cellar of the Hotel Adria, magically transformed a century ago into a fantastical undersea grotto. Sophisticated dining and impeccable service.
G8 Václavské náměstí 26 221 081 202 Můstek

U FLEKŮ (££)
Every visitor should sip the dark and tasty beer that has been brewed and served on these raucous premises for 200 years. There's also a big beer garden.
F9 Křemencova 11 224 934 019 Karlovo náměstí or Národní třída

U KALICHA (££)
Thanks to the Good Soldier Švejk's patronage in Austro-Hungarian days, this place is popular with visitors from abroad familiar with the famous Czech antihero. Solid food and accordion music among much Švejkian memorabilia.
G10 Na Bojišti 12–14 224 912 557 I P Pavlova

U PAŘAŠUTISTŮ (££)
World War II buffs will love this pub, a shrine to the Czechoslovak parachutists who assassinated Reichsprotektor Heydrich. Across the street is the museum devoted to them, located in the Sts. Cyril and Methodius Orthodox church.
F9 Resslova 7 737 670 278 Karlovo náměstí

U PINKASŮ (££)
This authentically restored pub was the first place in Prague to serve real Pilsner (in 1843). More refined dining upstairs, in what is one of the very best places to enjoy sustaining Bohemian specialties such as succulent roast duck.
G8 Jungmannovo náměstí 16 221 111 150 Můstek

EXOTIC TASTES

The Lemon Leaf (£–££) is a good choice for Thai and international cuisine. It is a short walk from Charles Square. Na Zderaze 14 224 919 056 Karlovo náměstí

U ŠUTERŮ (£££)
A cozy place specializing in Czech treats like roast duck, roast pork and fruit dumplings.
G8 Palackého 4, Nové Město 224 947 120 Closed dinner Můstek

VELRYBA (££)
The Whale opens wide its smoke-filled jaws to accommodate its trendy clientele.
F9 Opatovická 24 224 931 444 Národní třída

ZAHRADA V OPĚRE (££)
The place to dine after attending the Státní opera. Bright, light ambience, and delicious dishes from around the world.
H8 Legerova 75 (next to Radio Free Europe) 224 239 685 Muzeum

ZVONICE (££)
Unique ambience, high up in the belfry of St. Henry's Church. The food is as good as the view.
H8 Jindřišská věž, Jindřišská 224 220 009 Tram 3, 9, 14, 24 to Jindřišská

Hradčany

Hradčany takes its name from Prague Castle (Pražský hrad), the crag-top citadel commanding the bridges of the River Vltava. The district extends along the hilltop to Strahovský klášter.

4
5
6
7
8
B
C
Na valech
Minist Obrany
U Prašného mostu
Mariánské hradby
Královská zahrada
Oranžerie
Jelení
Brusnice
Pražský hrad
HRADČANY
Jizdarna Praž hradu
Jiřský klášter
U Brusnice
Bazilika a klášter sv Jiří
Nový Svět
Brusnice
Katedrála sv Víta
Šternberský palác
Všech svatých
Černínská
Kapucínská
sv Jan Nepomucký
Kanovnická
Martinický palác
Pražský hrad
Starý královský palác
Keplerova
U Kasáren
Arcibiskupský palác
Loreta
Hradčanské náměstí
Zám schody
Černínský palác
Loretánské náměstí
Schwarzenberský palác
Ke Hradu
Hládkov
Loretánská
Nerudova
Úvoz
Parléřova
Pohořelec
Lobkovická zahrada
Dlabačov
Strahovský klášter
Strahovská
Strahovská zahrada
0
250 m
250 yds

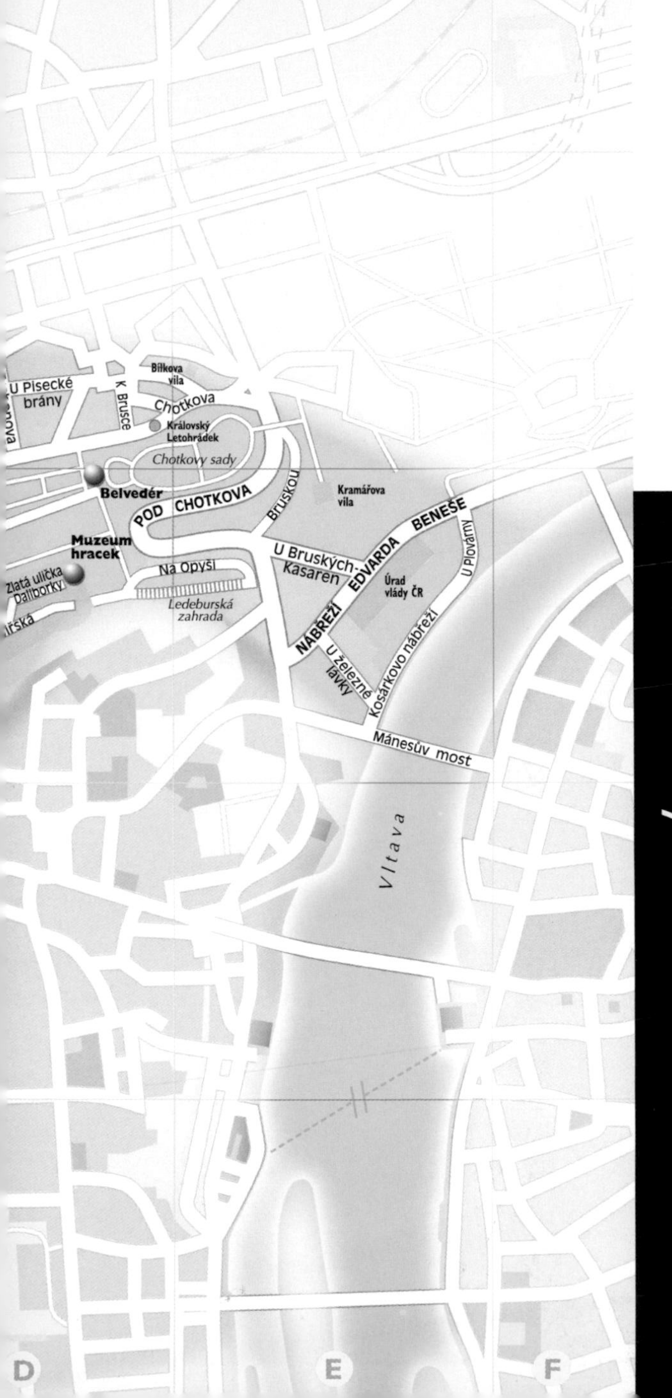

U Písecké brány
K Brusce
Bílkova vila
Chotkova
Královský Letohrádek
Chotkovy sady
Belvedér
POD CHOTKOVA
Bruskou
Kramářova vila
Muzeum hracek
Zlatá ulička Daliborky
Na Opyši
Ledeburská zahrada
U Bruských Kasaren
NÁBŘEŽÍ EDVARDA BENEŠE
U Plovárny
Úrad vlády ČR
U železné lávky
Kosárkovo nábřeží
Mánesův most
Vltava
D
E
F

Hradčany

Interior and exterior views of the Basilica of St. George

TOP 25

Bazilika a klášter sv Jiří

THE BASICS

www.ngprague.cz

D6

Jiřské náměstí

Gallery: 257 531 644

Basilica: Apr–Oct daily 9–5; rest of year daily 9–4.
Gallery: Tue–Sun 10–6

Restaurants and cafés in castle

Malostranská, then an uphill walk

Tram 22, 23 to Pražský hrad (Prague Castle)

Few

Moderate

HIGHLIGHTS

Basilica

- Gothic tomb of Prince Vratislav I
- St. Ludmila's chapel with frescos
- Renaissance south portal

Gallery

- Baroque Annunciation sculptures from East Bohemia
- Religious statuary by Jiří František Pacák and M. B. Braun
- *Tobias Restoring his Father's Sight* by Petr Brandl
- Landscapes by Roelandt Savery
- Genre scenes by Norbert Grund

A blood-red baroque façade conceals a severe ancient interior, the Romanesque Basilica of St. George. The nuns have long since left their convent to the north, now a setting for fine Czech Renaissance and baroque painting and sculpture.

Bare basilica The basilica is the biggest church of its date in the Czech provinces and its twin towers and pale, sober stonework are a reminder of the great antiquity of the Prague Castle complex. Very well preserved, it is now a concert venue. The austere interior, a great hall with wooden ceiling, houses a small but impressive collection of artworks.

Paintings and princesses Founded in 973, St. George's Convent was where princesses and other noble young ladies were sent for the best possible education. Shut down like many religious houses in 1782 by Emperor Joseph (who turned it into a barracks), it had to await the coming of the Communists for its rehabilitation; they planned to turn it into a museum of the Czechoslovak people. It now houses Mannerist, baroque and rococo painting and sculpture from the National Gallery's Old Bohemian collection. The comparatively small Mannerist holdings complement those at the Obrazárna (the Prague Castle Picture Gallery). The finest artworks here represent the Bohemian baroque, with massive sculpted saints writhing in ecstatic frenzy, while secular portraits and genre scenes illustrate local life.

Katedrála sv Víta

HIGHLIGHTS

- South Portal, with 14th-century mosaic
- St. Wenceslas's Chapel
- Crypt, with royal tombs
- Silver tomb of St. John Nepomuk
- West front sculptures

TIP

- You can get some idea of the glories of the cathedral by walking along the nave, which is free. To see its greatest treasures, like St Wenceslas's Chapel, you will need to buy a ticket at the entrance.

To emerge into Prague Castle's Third Courtyard and see the twin towers of St. Vitus's Cathedral lancing skyward is truly breathtaking. The sight is all the more compelling when you realize that this Gothic edifice was completed within living memory.

Spanning the centuries The cathedral was begun by Emperor Charles IV in the mid-14th century. It is built over the foundations of much earlier predecessors: a round church erected by 'Good King' (actually Prince) Wenceslas in the early 10th century and a big Romanesque building resembling the present-day Bazilika sv Jiří (▷ 67). The glory of the architecture is largely due to the Swabian builder Petr Parléř and his sons, who worked on the building for 60 years.

Clockwise from the left: detail of the Alfons Mucha art nouveau stained-glass window; the silver tomb of St. John Nepomuk; the spires of the cathedral dominate the rooftops of the Hradčany; the arched ceiling of the Chapel of the Holy Cross; exterior; bronze chandelier (1532) in the gilded Chapel of St. Wenceslas

Progress was halted abruptly by the troubles of the 15th century, and the cathedral consisted only of an east end until the formation of an 'Association for the Completion of the Cathedral', in 1843. Decades of effort saw the nave, western towers and much else brought to a triumphant conclusion; in 1929, a thousand years after Prince Wenceslas was assassinated, the cathedral was consecrated, dedicated to the country's patron saint, St. Vitus.

Cathedral treasures The cathedral is a treasure house of Bohemian history, though the Crown Jewels, its greatest prize, are seldom on display. The spacious interior absorbs the crowds with ease and provides a fitting context for an array of precious objects that range from medieval paintings to modern stained glass.

THE BASICS

www.svatyvit.cz
D6
Pražský hrad
257 531 052
Apr–Oct daily 9–5; rest of year daily 9–4. Tower: daily 9–4
Restaurants and cafés in castle
Tram 22, 23 to Pražský hrad (Prague Castle)
Fair
Newer section: free. Gothic section: moderate

Loreta

Church exterior (left); archway (middle); roof statue (below)

THE BASICS

www.loreta.cz
B6
Loretánské náměstí
220 516 740
Tue–Sun 9–12.15, 1–4.30
Tram 22, 23 to Pohořelec
Few
Moderate

HIGHLIGHTS

- The main façade, with statuary and carillon
- The Santa Casa
- Interior of the Church of the Nativity
- Diamond monstrance in the Loretto Treasury
- Cloister painting of St. Starosta

A bearded lady, skeletons rattling their bones to the sound of chiming bells, severed breasts and a flying house are not part of a freak show, but instead are all features of the sumptuous Loretto Shrine, on Hradčany Hill.

Counter-Reformation fireworks After the Battle of the White Mountain in 1620 Protestant austerity, with its repudiation of images, was replaced by the idolatry of the cult of the Virgin Mary, dripping with sensuality and symbolism. Of all the flights of architectural fantasy that the Roman Catholic Counter-Reformation perpetrated on Prague, the Loretto is the most bizarre as well as the most beautiful, its church and courtyard a theatre of cults, miracles and mysteries.

Weird wonders The kernel of the complex is a Santa Casa, a facsimile of the Virgin Mary's holy home in Nazareth, supposedly flown by angels from the Holy Land and deposited at Loreto in Italy. It is an ornate little Renaissance pavilion built in 1631 and later given an equally ornate baroque setting of courtyard, carillon tower and richly decorated church. Pilgrims once flocked here in huge numbers to marvel at the macabre: St. Agatha offering up her bloody bosom to the angels; the skeletons in their wax death masks; unhappy St. Starosta, whose father killed her in a fury after finding that she'd grown a beard to discourage a preferred suitor.

Displays of European art in the palace

TOP 25

Šternberský palác

Who would guess that the little alley beside the Prague archbishop's palace would lead to one of the nation's great art collections? Housed in the grand Šternberg Palace, it dazzles visitors with its old masters.

Ambitious aristocrats After building the Trojský zámek (Troja Château ▷ 98–99) on the edge of Prague, Count Šternberg, one of the city's richest men, needed a town house closer to Prague Castle. The Italian architect Giovanni Alliprandi designed the palace, and work began on the count's Hradčany home in 1698. However, the money ran out before the completion of the main façade. The interior was decorated with fine ceiling and wall paintings. It was a later Šternberg who donated much of the family's great picture collection to the precursor to the National Gallery in the early 19th century, and the nation's finest foreign paintings were housed here from 1821 to 1871. They are once more in this grand setting.

Picture palace Although tucked away behind Hradčanské náměstí, the Šternberg Palace is substantial, arranged around an imposing courtyard, with grand stairways and an oval pavilion facing the garden. The paintings of the National Gallery of European Art could keep an art lover busy for a day, though some star exhibits are no longer on view: A policy of restitution has returned them to the owners from whom they were confiscated by the Communists.

THE BASICS

www.ngprague.cz
- C6
- Hradčanské náměstí
- 233 090 570;
- Tue–Sun 10–6
- Café
- Tram 22, 23 to Pražský hrad
- Few
- Moderate

HIGHLIGHTS

- Triptych of the Adoration of the Magi, Giertgen tot Sint Jans
- *Adam and Eve*, Cranach
- *Feast of the Rosary*, Dürer
- *Scholar in his Study*, Rembrandt
- *Head of Christ*, El Greco
- Portraits from 2nd-century Egypt
- *Beheading of St. Dorothy*, Hans Baldung Grien
- *Eleonora of Toledo*, Bronzino
- *St. Jerome*, Ribera

Pražský hrad

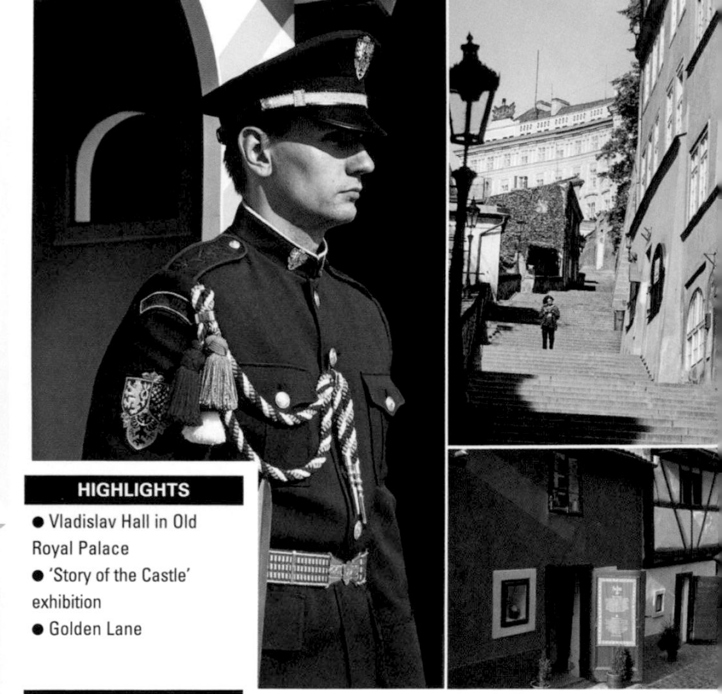

HIGHLIGHTS

- Vladislav Hall in Old Royal Palace
- 'Story of the Castle' exhibition
- Golden Lane

TIPS

- The best time to see the Changing of the Guard at the western entrance is at midday, when there is a more elaborate ceremony, enhanced by a musical accompaniment.
- Buy tickets for the Castle interiors (and Golden Lane) at the information office, and bear in mind that separate tickets must be purchased for the Cathedral's crypt, choir and chapels and to see the artworks in St. George's Convent.

The thousand windows of Prague Castle gaze over the city. This is the citadel of the Czech nation and it holds its collective memory. It includes palaces, churches, streets, squares and treasures.

Castle denizens At the castle's western gates, blue-uniformed guardsmen stand to attention beneath a pair of battling Baroque giants. Beyond, a series of courtyards echo with the tread of countless ghosts: from emperors like Charles IV and Rudolph II to the rulers of modern times.

Exploring the castle The castle offers plenty of attractions. In the Starý královský palác/Old Royal Palace, the gloriously vaulted Vladislavský sál/Vladislav Hall is spacious

Clockwise from left: a guard in his box at Prague Castle; descending the Zamecke schody (New Castle Steps); detail of No 13 Golden Lane (Zlatá ulička); Golden Lane built into the fortifications of the castle; looking across the river towards Malá Strana and the castle; cobbled Golden Lane

enough to have served for tournaments. In 1618, from an adjacent room, the Prague Defenestration took place, when Catholic councillors were thrown out into the moat, though a dungheap broke their fall. Their survival is marked by a monument in the gardens along the southern ramparts. The northern ramparts can be explored, too, and built into their walls are the brightly painted 'alchemists' cottages' of Zlatá ulička/Golden Lane. To immerse yourself in the past of the castle, descend into its labyrinthine substructure, which now houses 'The Story of the Castle', a succession of fascinating, state-of-the-art displays. Children will enjoy the Muzeum hraček/Toy Museum just off Jiřská ulička, the lane leading down to the Černá věž/Black Tower guarding the eastern entrance to the citadel.

THE BASICS

www.hrad.cz
C/D6
Pražský hrad
224 373 300/368
Courtyards and streets: daily until late. Buildings: Apr–Oct daily 9–5; rest of year 9–4
Cafés and restaurants
Malostranská, then an uphill walk
Tram 22, 23 to Pražský hrad
Few
Moderate

Strahovský klášter

HIGHLIGHTS

- 17th-century Theological Hall
- 18th-century Philosophical Hall
- Strahovská obrazárna (Strahov Picture Gallery)
- 9th-century Strahov Gospels

TIP

- Strahov has a Cabinet of Curiosities in its lobby, the weird and wonderful objects here matched by the microscopic oddities in the Muzeum Miniatur on the far side of the courtyard.

Baroque spires rising to Heaven, a gilded image of an enemy of the Faith, monks profiting from an enterprise in Hell: The Strahov Monastery seems to encapsulate something of this paradoxical city.

Persuasive priests The Strahov Monastery, a landmark in the cityscape, crowns the steep slope up from Malá Strana. It is a treasure-house of literature, and its ornate library halls, with their splendid frescos, are among the most magnificent in Europe. As befits a monastery devoted to books, Strahov owed much to its abbots' ways with words. Its 12th-century founder, Abbot Zdík, persuaded Prince Vladislav II to back his project by making flattering comparisons of Prague with the holy city of Jerusalem. Much later, in 1783, Abbot Meyer

From the left: detail of the ceiling fresco depicting the Banquet of King Balthasar, decorating the ceiling of the former abbot's dining room; the exterior of the monastery, with the statue of St. Norbert on the top; the 9th-century Strahov Gospel, with a richly bejewelled cover, in the monastery

exercised equal powers of persuasion on Emperor Joseph II to exempt Strahov from his edict that closed down many of the Habsburg Empire's monasteries. The cleric was so eloquent that Strahov benefited from the misfortune of other institutions: Books from the suppressed monastery at Louka were brought here by the wagonload. A gilded medallion of the emperor over the library entrance may also have helped to persuade Joseph that the Strahov monks deserved special treatment.

Returnees' revenge The monks, of the Premonstratensian Order, were chased out of Strahov by the Communists in 1952, but have come back. The upper floor of the cloisters is a gallery for the art returned to them; a wine cellar is now a restaurant called Peklo (Hell).

THE BASICS

www.
strahovskyklaster.cz
B7
Strahovské nádvoří 1
220 516 671
Library halls: daily 9–noon, 1–5. Gallery: Tue–Sun 9–noon, 12.30–5
Peklo (Hell) restaurant in monastery cellars
Tram 22, 23 to Pohořelec
Fair
Moderate

More to See

ARCIBISKUPSKÝ PALÁC (ARCHBISHOP'S PALACE)

The lusciously restored rococo façade hides a sumptuous residence, unfortunately accessible only on special occasions.

C6 Hradčanské náměstí 16 Not normally open to public Trams 22, 23 to Pražský hrad

BELVEDÉR

Also known as the Královský letohrádek (Royal Summer Palace), the Belvedere at the eastern end of the Royal Garden was built in the mid-16th century by Ferdinand I for his beloved consort, Queen Anna. With its elegant arcade and its roof in the shape of an upturned boat, it was one of the first buildings in Central Europe to be inspired by the ideas of the Italian Renaissance. It is used for temporary exhibitions. In the middle of the formal garden setting off the Belvedér stands the Singing Fountain, which gets its name from the resonance made by the water falling into its basin.

D5 Mariánské hradby 52 224 372 327 Open only for temporary exhibitions Tram 22, 23 to Královský letohrádek

ČERNÍNSKÝ PALÁC (ČERNÍN PALACE)

This monstrous mass of masonry, one of the biggest of all Prague's palaces, was begun by Jan Humprecht, Count Czernin, in 1669, bankrupting his family for generations to come. Eventually it became a barracks, then the country's Foreign Ministry. Reichsprotektor Heydrich lorded it here during the Nazi occupation, then in 1948, after the Communist coup, it was here that another Prague defenestration took place, that of democratic Foreign Minister Jan Masaryk.

B7 Loretánské náměstí Not open to the public Tram 22, 23 to Pohořelec

KRÁLOVSKÁ ZAHRADA (ROYAL GARDENS)

The trees and lawns of the Royal

Exterior of the 18th-century Sternberský Palác (▷ 71)

The Renaissance façade of Černín Palace, reflected on the roof of a car

Gardens stretch out along the plateau on the far side of the Stag Moat defending the northern flank of the Castle. Long ago they housed the Imperial zoo, whose denizens included lions, tigers and even a dodo. Europe's first tulips were grown here. Nowadays the gardens offer an escape from the crowds, as well as providing unusual views of the Castle and Cathedral. Apart from the lovely Belvedér (▷ 76), the most fascinating structure in the gardens is the mid-16th-century Míčovna (Ball Game Hall); if you look hard among its sgraffito decoration you can find a hammer and sickle, clandestinely inserted in Communist times.

C/D6 ✉ Královská zahrada
Apr–Oct daily 10–6 Tram 22, 23 to Královský letohrádek or Pražský hrad
Free

NOVÝ SVĚT

A world away from the pomp of Hradčany's palaces, this rustic little quarter is like a piece of countryside left over from the city's expansion. Basically consisting of a single winding lane, Nový Svět (New World) itself has become a popular enclave of artists and intellectuals and has resisted commercialization. In the past, its picturesque dwellings housed the castle's servants, as well as rather more eminent clients of the royal household like astronomer Tycho Brahe and mathematician Johannes Kepler.

B/C6 ✉ Nový Svět
Restaurant at No. 3
Tram 22, 23 to Brusnice Few

SCHWARZENBERSKÝ PALÁC (SCHWARZENBERG PALACE)

The city's most imposing Renaissance palace is just outside Prague Castle, its sgraffito-bedecked façade and bristling gables making a noble impression. It is the future home for collections of the National Gallery.

C6 ✉ Hradčanské náměstí 2 ☎ 222 202 398 Closed for reconstruction
Trams 22, 23 to Pražský hrad

Courtyard of the Museum of Military History in the Schwarzenberský Palác

Street sign and lamp on Nový Svět

Hradčany to Malá Strana

After exploring the byways of Hradčany, this walk follows an unusual route down to Malá Strana.

DISTANCE: 3km (2 miles) **ALLOW:** 1.5 hours

START

STRAHOVSKÝ KLÁŠTER

B7 Tram 22, 23 to Pohořelec

❶ At the courtyard of Strahovský klašter, turn right down steps which pass beneath the buildings.

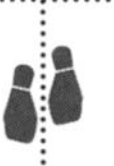

❷ Turn right on emerging into the square, take the left fork and turn left downhill to the Loreta. Bear left across the square and walk down the lane of Černínská.

❸ This brings you to Nový Svět, where you turn right and walk along the winding cobbled street which brings you eventually into palace-lined Hradčanské náměstí.

❹ Enter the castle at the western entrance and walk to the Third Courtyard on the southern side of the cathedral. At the far end of the courtyard descend the stairway, to emerge into the gardens in the southern ramparts.

❺ Turn left and walk along the ramparts, enjoying the view down into Malá Strana.

❻ At the Moravská bašta, marked by a slim column, go down the steps and buy a ticket for the Zahrady pod Pražským hradem (Gardens beneath the Castle).

❼ The exit from the gardens brings you into Valdštejnské náměstí (Wallenstein Square), dominated by the great palace built by General Wallenstein, now the home of the Senate.

❽ Turn right along Tomášská, which brings you into Malostranské náměstí, with its busy tram stop.

END

MALOSTRANSKÉ NÁMĚSTÍ

D7 Tram 12, 20, 22, 23

Shopping

CDMUSIC.CZ

A small and welcoming record establishment in the arcade on the south side of Loretto Square, specializing in 'Czech Labels at Czech Prices'. It stocks a comprehensive array of Czech classical music as well as some of the wonderful jazz produced in Prague.
B7 Široký dvůr, Loretánské náměstí 220 515 403 Tram 22, 23 to Pohořelec

GAMBRA

The little Nový Svět gallery has intriguing art objects and books.
B6 Černínská 5 Tram 22, 23 to Brusnice 22, 23 to Pohořelec

MUSEUM SHOP

Unusually tasteful and original souvenirs based on the treasures of the many Prague museums, plus foreign art books not available elsewhere in Prague. An example to other souvenir shops worldwide; where else, for example, could you buy a china mug with elegant sgraffito patterning?
C6 Jiřská 6, Hradčany 224 373 264 Tram 22, 23 to Pražský hrad

ZLATÁ ULIČKA (GOLDEN LANE)

Even though you have to pay to get in (tickets from the Castle ticket office), picturesque Golden Lane, with its line of quaint and cheerful little cottages, is worth visiting if you are in search of unusual souvenirs. The tiny buildings are now shops selling a variety of items, among them (at No. 23) a fascinating selection of antique prints and maps.
D6 Zlatá ulička, Pražský hrad

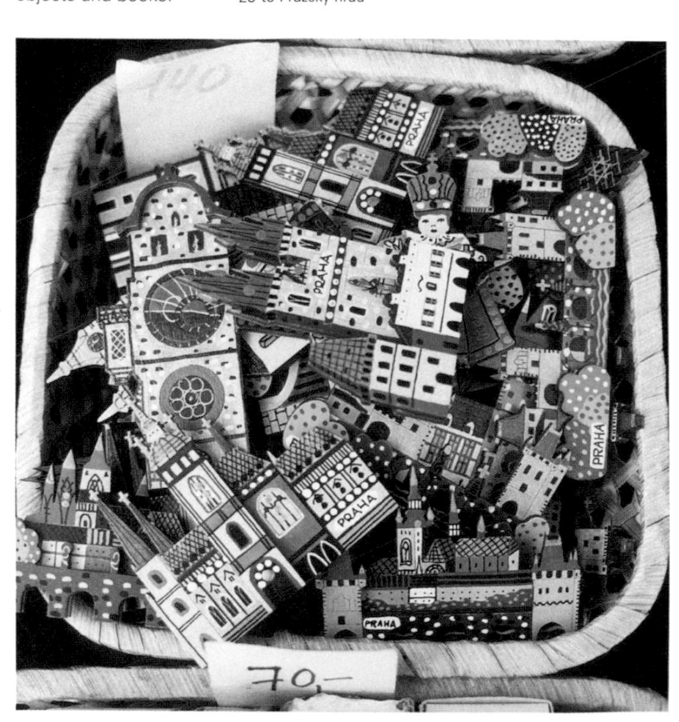

Restaurants

PRICES

Prices are approximate, based on a 3-course meal for one person.

£££ over £800Kč
££ 400Kč–£800Kč
£ under 400Kč

BELLAVISTA (££)
Reopened as part of the reputable Kolkovna group, the Bellavista more than lives up to its new name; perched on the edge of the Strahov Monastery, it has a summer terrace with a glorious panorama over Prague. The cuisine is international with an Italian touch.
B7 Strahovské nádvoří 1 220 517 274 Tram 22, 23 to Pohořelec

LOBKOWICZ PALACE CAFÉ (£)
This aristocratic establishment occupies a couple of tastefully decorated rooms in a private palace forming part of the castle complex. It's easily the best place hereabouts for a snack or light meal, especially if you sit out on the balcony overlooking the castle gardens.
D6 Jiřská 3, Pražský hrad 602 595 998 Malostranská, or tram 22, 23 to Pražský hrad

LVÍ DVŮR (££)
In a strategic setting on the northern approach to the castle, the historic 'Lion Court' uses its name to evoke the wild beasts once kept here in the imperial zoo. Meat such as venison features on the menu, though the specialty is a whole suckling pig cooked on a spit.
C6 U Pražného mostu 6 224 372 226 Tram 22, 23 to Pražský hrad

U CÍSAŘŮ (££)
This ancient building has an ambience worthy of its name 'At the Emperor's'. The atmospheric, vaulted rooms include arms and armour, aristocratic portraits, and the occasional bearskin. The menu is international and Czech cuisine.
C7 Loretánská 5 220 518 484 Tram 22, 23 to Pohořelec

U ZLATÉ HRUŠKY (£££)
Serving traditional Bohemian dishes as well as more international fare, the 'Golden Pear' occupies a lovely old baroque residence on the charming lane of Nový Svět. It also has an attractive garden section.
C7 Nový Svět 3 220 514 778 Tram 22, 23 to Brusnice

BEWARE

Prague waiters have largely overcome a reputation for overcharging. But it makes sense to check your bill carefully before paying. A common (and acceptable) practice is the offer before the meal of tempting hors d'oeuvres. These aren't complimentary, and you will have to pay for them.

U ZLATÉ STUDNĚ (££)
Pressed up against the southern ramparts of the castle, the restored 'Golden Well' is one of Prague's most prestigious hotels and restaurants. Strictly speaking it is part of Malá Strana, but is included here for its lovely outdoor café reached by going down a few steps from the Castle's south gardens.
D6 U Zlaté studně 166 257 011 213 Malostranská, or tram 22, 23 to Pražský hrad

VIKÁRKA (££)
The historic quarters once lived in by the cathedral's curates are partly occupied by this reopened restaurant. With its traditional ambience and its interesting take on old Czech dishes, it's perhaps the best place in the Castle precincts to interrupt your sightseeing with a substantial meal.
D6 Vikářská 39, Pražský hrad 233 311 962 Tram 22, 23 to Pražský hrad

Perched below the Castle, Mala Strana (Lesser Town) is Prague's most prefectly preserved historic district, an area of palaces and gardens, now peppered with chic restaurants and smart hotels.

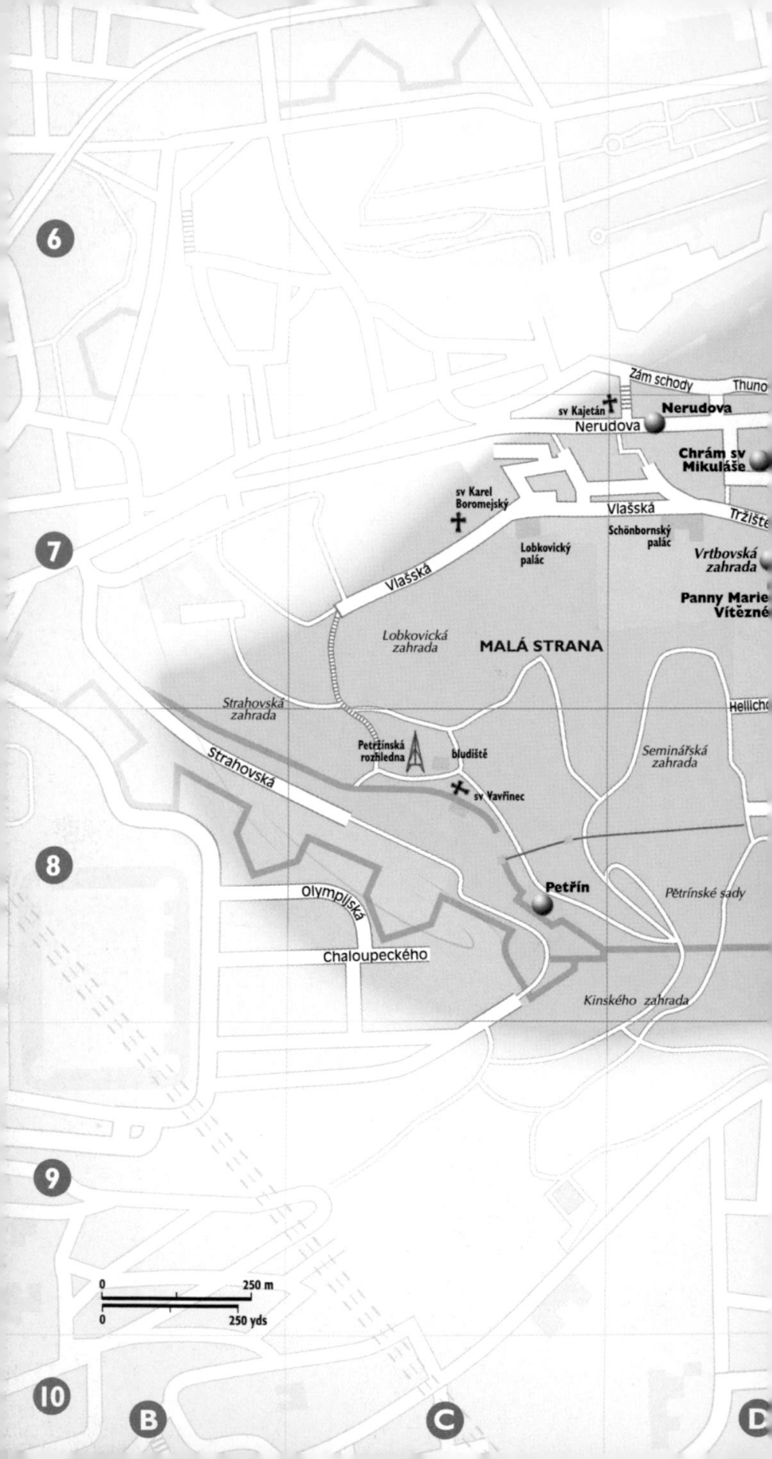

6
7
8
9
10
B
C
D
Zám schody
Thuno
sv Kajetán
Nerudova
Nerudova
Chrám sv Mikuláše
sv Karel Boromejský
Vlašská
Tržiště
Schönbornský palác
Lobkovický palác
Vrtbovská zahrada
Vlašská
Panny Marie Vítězné
Lobkovická zahrada
MALÁ STRANA
Strahovská zahrada
Hellich
Petřínská rozhledna
bludiště
Seminářská zahrada
Strahovská
sv Vavřinec
Petřín
Pětrínské sady
Olympijská
Chaloupeckého
Kinského zahrada
0
250 m
0
250 yds

Ledeburská zahrada
Zahrady pod Pražským hradem
Valdštejnská
Ledeburský palác
Malostranská
Senát
Valdštejnský palác
Letenská
Tomášská
sv Tomáše
Vojanovy sady
Mánesův most
Minist financí
Franz Kafka Museum
Malostranské náměstí
sv Josefa
U Lužického semináře
Cihelná
Malostranské náměstí
Josefská
Muzeum
Mišenská
Mostecká
Lázeňská
Saská
Karlův most
Prokopská
Panny Marie pod řetězem
Hroznová
Na Kampě
Lichtenštejnský palác
Hellichova
Nosticova
KAMPA
Muzeum hudby
Muzeum Kampa
U Sovových
Tyršovo muzeum
Čertovka
Kampa
Vltava
Újezd
Všehrdova
sv Jana na pradle
Malostranské nábřeží
Říční
Újezd
Vítězná
most Legií
Plaská
Zborovská
Janáčkovo nábřeží
Mělnická
E
F

Chrám sv Mikuláše

TOP 25

HIGHLIGHTS

Chrám sv Mikuláše

- West front
- St. Barbara's Chapel
- Organ with fresco of St. Cecilia
- Dome with Holy Trinity fresco
- Huge sculptures of four Church Fathers
- Trompe-l'oeil ceiling fresco by Kracker

TIP

- The 215 steps of the bell tower of St. Nicholas's Church (entrance on south side of the building) are well worth climbing; from the top there are fantastic views, including close-ups of the church's dome and statuary as well as of the whole of Malá Strana and the city beyond.

As you walk around the base of the lofty St. Nicholas's Church, you feel the power of the Catholic Counter-Reformation expressed in one of the most beautiful baroque buildings of Central Europe.

Counter-Reformation citadel When the Jesuits came to Prague following the route of the Protestants at the Battle of the White Mountain, the existing little 13th-century church at the middle of Malostranské náměstí (Malá Strana Square) was far too modest for their aspirations. The new St. Nicholas's Church was eventually completed in the 18th century and, with its lofty walls and high dome and bell tower, became one of the dominant features of the city. The Jesuits intended their church to impress, but not through size alone.

Clockwise from left: the frescos decorating the walls and cupola; view from the church across the Vltava river to the towers of Týn Church, Powder Gate and St. Nicholas; the curving façade and green copper dome and tower of the church; the magnificent interior

They employed the finest architects of the day (the Dientzenhofers, father and son, plus Anselmo Lurago), along with talented interior designers. Inside, no effort was spared to enthral via the dynamic play of space, statuary and painting, a fantastically decorated pulpit and a 2,500-pipe organ (played by Mozart on several occasions).

Princely palaces and humbler households In front of the huge church swirls the life of Malá Strana—locals waiting for the trams mixing with visitors following the Royal Way up to Hradčany. Malostranské náměstí is lined with a fascinating mixture of ancient town houses and grand palaces, while attached to St. Nicholas's is the Jesuits's college, now part of the university.

THE BASICS

www.psalterium.cz
D7
Malostranské náměstí
257 534 215
Mar–Oct daily 9–5; rest of year daily 9–4. Tower: Apr–early Nov daily 10–5
Restaurants and cafés in square
Malostranská
Tram 12, 20, 22, 23 to Malostranské náměstí
Few
Inexpensive

Malostranské náměstí

Bar sign (left); Lobkovický palác (German embassy, middle); aerial view

THE BASICS

D7
Malostranské náměstí
Tram 12, 20, 22, 23 to Malostranské náměstí

TIP

- The square offers exciting possibilities for taking photographs at all times of day and night. Floodlighting transforms the great presence of the Church of St. Nicholas, especially when framed by the square's arcades.

Overlooked by the city's greatest baroque church Chrám sv Mikuláše (Church of St. Nicholas), Malá Strana Square is the hub of the Lesser Town and a focal point on the route between the Old Town and the castle.

A place to relax There's plenty to see and explore in and around the square and nearby streets and lanes. It's here in the heart of Malá Strana (Lesser Town) that most visitors pause before tackling the steep climb up to the Castle, not least because of the temptation offered by the bars, cafés and restaurants.

The buildings St. Nicholas divides the sloping square into an upper and a lower half, each lined by the palaces and patrician houses so characteristic of this part of town. Some are very old, but most were rebuilt or given new façades in baroque style in the late 17th and 18th centuries. The grandest of the aristocratic edifices is the Lichtenštejnský palác (Lichtenstein Palace), which takes up the whole of the western side of the square. Built on the orders of Karl von Lichtenstein (1569–1627), it now houses the music faculty of the university. Take time to admire the broad arcades of the burgher's houses along the south of the square, and peer into the entrance of No. 1/272, a fine example of an old-fashioned Prague *pavlač* (galleried courtyard); it has the enchanting name of U petržílka (Parsley House).

View to Vltava from the Petřín Tower (below); the Mirror Maze on the hill

TOP 25

Petřín

When the crowds on Charles Bridge become too much, there's always the glorious green of Petřín Hill, its orchards and woodlands a cool retreat from the middle of the city—and a real breath of the countryside in the metropolis.

A train with a view In 1891, for the city's great Jubilee Expo that celebrated the achievements of the Czech provinces when they still formed part of the Austrian Empire, the city leaders provided a jolly little funicular railway (the 'Lanovka') to the top of Petřín Hill. Now restored, it once again carries passengers effortlessly up the steep slope. At the top there's a whole array of attractions, including the Rozhledna ('Lookout'), the little brother of the Eiffel Tower, also built in 1891. Its 299 steps lead to a viewing platform offering a fantastic panorama over the city. Next to the tower, the old-fashioned Mirror Maze (Bludiště) continues to work its hilarious magic. In the same building is an equally old-fashioned but effective diorama depicting an historic battle on Charles Bridge.

Country matters With its woods and orchards (splendid in spring), Petřín provides a welcome counterpoint to the busy castle area. Once there were vineyards on the hill, but these didn't survive the Thirty Years War in the 17th century. They were replaced by the superb gardens that link the palaces of Malá Strana to the surrounding hillside parklands.

THE BASICS

C/D 7–8
Rozhledna, Mirror Maze: May, Jun, Sep daily 10–10; Apr daily 10–7; Jul–Aug daily 10–8; Oct daily 10–6; Nov–Mar Sat–Sun 10–5
Restaurant and café
Funicular railway, from Újezd in Malá Strana
Tram 22, 23 to Pohořelec then walk
Few
Rozhledna, Mirror Maze: inexpensive

HIGHLIGHTS

- Rozhledna viewing tower
- 4th-century Hunger Wall
- Mirror Maze (Bludiště)
- Charles Bridge Battle diorama

Valdštejnský palác

Statues in the formal garden (left); relief work on a heavy brass palace door

THE BASICS

www.senat.cz
D/E6
Palace: Valdštejnské náměstí.
Garden: Letenská 10
Palace: Sat, Sun 9–4.
Garden: daily 10–6
Malostranská
Fair
Free

HIGHLIGHTS

- Sala Terrena
- Garden sculptures (copies of originals by de Vries)
- Grotesquery and aviary in garden

Think of Wallenstein Palace—Prague's biggest palace—as an awful warning to eschew the excessive ambition of its builder, Albrecht von Wallenstein, whose desire for power led to his assassination.

Greedy generalissimo Wallenstein's huge late Renaissance/early baroque palace crouches at the foot of Prague Castle as if waiting greedily to gobble it up. A whole city block was demolished to make way for the complex of five courtyards, a barracks, a riding school and a superb garden that were intended to reflect Wallenstein's wealth and status. Wallenstein (Valdštejn in Czech) turned the troubled early 17th century to his advantage. Having wormed his way into the emperor's good graces, he became governor of Prague, then Duke of Friedland. He married for money (twice), and great tracts of land (even towns) fell into his hands following the Battle of the White Mountain in 1620. His fortune grew more as he quartermastered the imperial armies as well as leading them. Rightly suspicious of his subject's intentions, the emperor had him killed.

The general's garden The great hall of the palace canbe seen only on special occasions, as the Czech Senate now occupies the building. More freely accessible, the formal garden is dominated by the superb Sala Terrena loggia, modelled on those in Italy, and has convincing copies of the statues stolen by Swedish soldiers during the Thirty Years War.

More to See

FRANZ KAFKA MUSEUM

For all those who feel they should know more about the famous writer, this innovative exhibition is the answer. It also has an excellent shop with unusual souvenirs.

E7 Cihelná 2B 221 451 414
Daily 10–6 Malostranská

MUZEUM HUDBY

www.nm.cz

The National Museum of Music, in the stimulating setting of a Malá Strana church, exhibits instruments and memorabilia that more than do justice to this musical nation. After costly conversion, the nave now functions as a fine concert hall, overlooked by several floors of side galleries in which the collections are expertly displayed. Every conceivable type of instrument is on show, from violins once owned by virtuosos to some extremely odd-looking bagpipes, a Czech speciality. Even odder are the bulbous brass instruments arranged in artful patterns in their showcases.

D7 Karmelitská 2/4 257 327 285
Wed–Mon 10–6 Moderate
Tram 12, 20, 22, 23 to Hellichová

MUZEUM KAMPA

www.muzeumkampa.cz

This superb conversion of an historic mill houses an important collection of modern Czech art.

E8 U Sovoých mlýnů 2 257 286 147 Daily 10–6 Riverside restaurant and café Trams 12, 20, 22, 23 to Hellichova Moderate

NERUDOVA

One of Prague's loveliest streets, Nerudova forms part of the Royal Route, rising steeply from Malá Strana Square towards the castle. The climb reveals one delight after another: Baroque town houses with elaborate house signs proclaiming their names ('The Three Little Fiddles', 'The Golden Key'), stately palaces with portals guarded by pairs of eagles or muscular moors. House No. 47 ('The Two Suns) was the home of the 19th-century writer

Baroque and Renaissance buildings lining Nerudova

Jan Neruda, who depicted the doings of the denizens of Malá Strana with a Dickensian pen.

C/D7 Nerudova Restaurants and cafés Trams 12, 22, 23 to Malostranské náměstí Few

PANNY MARIE VÍTĚZNÉ

www.pragjesu.info

The Church of Our Lady of Victory welcomes pilgrims from all over the world, who come to venerate the wax figurine known as the Bambino di Praga. Originally dedicated to the Holy Trinity, the church was given its present name following the 1620 Battle of the White Mountain, when it was handed over to the Spanish Carmelite order. In 1628 the church was given the little figure of the infant Jesus, which became the focus of a widespread cult.

D7 Karmelitská 9 257 533 646 Church: Mon–Sat 8.30–6.30, Sun 9.30–8 (hours may vary). Museum: Mon–Sat 10–5.30, Sun 1–5 Free Tram 12, 20, 22, 23 to Hellichova or Malostranské náměstí

VRTBOVSKÁ ZAHRADA (VRTBA GARDEN)

www.vrtbovska.cz

Prague's finest individual baroque garden has sculptures and a view over Malá Strana.

D4 Karmelitská 25 257 531 480 Apr–Oct daily 10–6 Tram 12, 20, 22, 23 to Malostranské náměstí Inexpensive

ZAHRADY POD PRAŽSKÝM HRADEM

This glorious group of terraced (formerly private) gardens of artistocratic families, clings to the near-vertical slope dropping from the castle ramparts to the palaces lining Valdštejnská street. Apart from their intrinsic attractiveness, they form an intriguing alternative route to and from the Hradčany heights (though only in season).

D6 Valdštejnské náměstí 3 257 010 401/257 530 467 Apr–end Oct daily 10–6 (last entry 5.30pm) Inexpensive Malostranská Tram 12, 20, 22, 23 to Malostranské náměstí

Trees frame the Church of Our Lady of Victory

The slender green-copper spire of the Church of St. Thomas

Malá Strana

This walk allows you to discover some of the less frequented parts of Prague's best-preserved historic district.

DISTANCE: 3.5km (2 miles) **ALLOW:** 2 hours

START

MALOSTRANSKÁ METRO

E6 Malostranská

❶ From the station find your way to the upstream approach to Mánes Bridge. Turn right down steps into the little riverside park from where there are unusual Old Town views.

❷ At the far end of the park, turn left into Cihelná. The street is named after an old brickworks, now a restaurant. The Kafka Museum is in its courtyard.

❸ Continue in the same direction, bearing left over Čertovka (Devil's Brook), and pass beneath one of the arches of the Charles Bridge.

❹ You are now in Kampa Island. At the start of parkland go right to recross Čertovka. Bear right at the end of the park and follow a narrow street to Maltézské náměstí (Maltese Square).

❺ Walk across and head left into Prokopsá at the far end, and turn right along busy Karmelistská.

❻ Cross the road and walk up Tržiště. Continue uphill, bearing left into Vlašská. The magnificent Lobkovický palác houses the German Embassy.

❼ Go up little Šporkova opposite the German Emabssy and follow it round, turning left up steps that bring you onto one of Prague's loveliest streets, Nerudova. Turn right and walk slowly downhill past baroque and rococo town houses.

❽ Nerudova leads down into upper Malostranské náměstí. The busy tram stop is in the lower part of the square.

END

MALOSTRANSKÉ NÁMĚSTÍ

D7 Tram 12, 20, 22, 23

Shopping

AHASVER ANTIQUES

An unusual little establishment with an intriguing line in vintage apparel, lace, linen and accessories.
D7 Prokopska 3 257 531 40 Tue–Sun 11–6 Tram 12, 20, 22, 23 to Hellichova or Malostranské náměstí

KOŽEŠINY KUBÍN

A modest alternative to the grandiose Liska shop in the Old Town, this is a privately run little fur and leather shop.
D8 Vítězná 12 257 323 600 Mon–Fri 9–6, Sat 9–1 Újezd

OBCHOD S LOUTKAMI

Head here when not just any marionette will do. Some of the finest handmade puppets available in Prague. Some of the individual designs can be expensive but others are reasonably priced. Supplied by over 30 different craftsmen.
D7 Nerudova 47 and 51 257 532 735 Daily 10–6 Tram 12, 20, 22, 23 to Malostranské náměstí

PAVLA A OLGA

Original and innovative fashion from acclaimed fashion designers.
C7 Vlašská 13 728 939 872 PM only Tram 12, 20, 22, 23 to Malostranské náměstí

U ZLATÉ ČÍŠE

As well as secondhand books, this treasure cave of an antiquarian bookshop has a changing stock of old posters, postcards, prints and banknotes, and even a limited number of miniature versions of the distinctive Prague street signs and house numbers.
D7 Nerudova 16 257 531 393 Daily 10–6 Tram 12, 20, 22, 23 to Malostranské náměstí

Entertainment and Nightlife

CHRÁM SV MIKULÁŠE (ST. NICHOLAS'S CHURCH)

The organ that Mozart played in Prague's greatest baroque church still accompanies choral concerts.
D7 Malostranské náměstí 25 257 534 215 Tram 12, 20, 22, 23 to Malostranské náměstí

LICHTENŠTEJNSKÝ PALÁC (LIECHTENSTEIN PALACE)

Setting for symphonic and other performances. The home of the Prague Music Academy where students perform regularly.
D7 Malostranské náměstí 13 257 534 206 Tram 12, 20, 22, 23 to Malostranské náměstí

PRAGUE PUPPETS

Puppetry has a long tradition in the Czech lands, and puppets are certainly not just for children. Collectors pay good money for hand-carved marionettes, and there are several theatres that bring these dolls to life. Among the most-loved figures are those of the serio-comic duo of Speibl (father) and son Hurvínek.

U MALÉHO GLENA

Little Glenn's is named after its genial owner, who plays recorded jazz in the upstairs bar and the real thing—alternating with pop or rock—in the basement.
D7 Karmelitská 23 257 531 717 Tram 12, 20, 22, 23 to Malostranské náměstí

Restaurants

PRICES

Prices are approximate, based on a 3-course meal for one person.
£££ over £800Kč
££ 400Kč–£800Kč
£ under 400Kč

ALCHYMIST (£££)
Opened in 2004, with an intimate but sumptuous interior to complement its inventive cuisine.
D7 Hellichova 4 257 312 518 Tram 12, 20, 22, 23 to Hellichova

BOHEMIA BAGEL (£)
A long-established hang-out for North American expats and visitors, the Bagel serves classic breakfasts, hearty soups and well-filled rolls, as well as abundant coffee.
D8 Újezd 16 257 310 694 Tram 6, 9, 12, 20, 22, 23 to Újezd

CAFÉ EBEL (£)
A post-1989 institution, known for its excellent coffee, the Ebel has expanded from its original location in the Týn Courtyard. One of five branches, this is in the Hergetová Cihelna complex.
E7 Cihelna 2B 257 535 299 Malostranská

CAFÉ SAVOY (££)
Kafka hung out here when it was a humble café. Now more classy, it's gaining a reputation for its French-inspired cuisine and fresh seafood.
D8 Vítězná 5 257 311 562 Tram 6, 9, 22, 23 to Újezd

ČERNÝ OREL (£)
An enclosed courtyard and rustic interior lend this inn the feeling of being removed from the bustling city streets.
E7 U Lužického semináře 40 257 531 738 Malostranská

CODA (£££)
Irresistible international dishes served in the stunning ambience of the covered courtyard of the Aria Hotel, or on a rooftop terrace in summer.
D7 Tržiště 9 225 334 790 Tram 12, 20, 22, 23 to Malostranské náměstí

TURKISH COFFEE

Espresso, cappuccino and most other coffee can now be found in Prague, but don't be surprised if you get served a traditional *turecká káva.* This is Czech-style Turkish coffee—that is, hot water pured right over ground coffee. Invariably served in a piping-hot glass with no handle. Be sure to stop swallowing—that is before you disturb the deposit of coffee grounds at the bottom of the cup

DAVID (£££)
An intimate setting and faultless food, including melt-in-the-mouth lamb, a house specialty.
D7 Tržiště 21 257 533 109 Tram 12, 20, 22, 23 to Malostranské náměstí

GITANES (£)
This intimate little restaurant, with its décor of naïve paintings, transports you deep into the Balkans, with fiery food washed down with a selection of Mediterranean wines.
D7 Tržiště 7 257 530 163 Tram 12, 20, 22, 23 to Malostranské náměstí

HERGETOVA CIHELNA (£££)
Stylishly converted historic brickworks with an intriguing contemporary interior and riverside terrace. Equally stylish, contemporary fare.
E7 Cihelná 2b 257 535 534 Malostranská

HUNGARIAN GROTTO (££)
For a change from Czech cuisine, descend into the venerable brick vaults of this historic establishment, where spicy Magyar dishes are served with wines from the Hungarian plains and the shores of Lake Balaton.

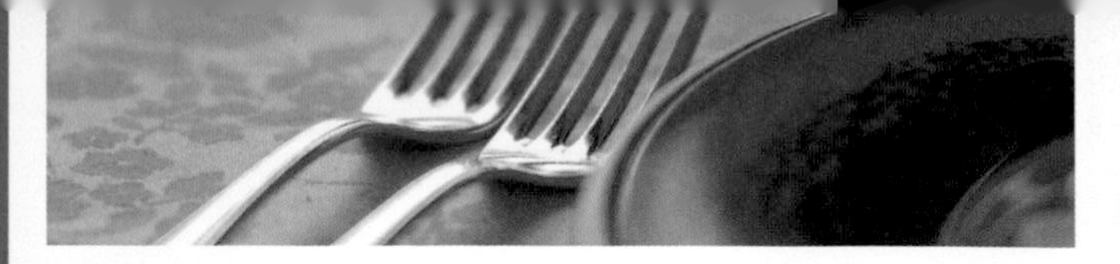

PRICES

Prices are approximate, based on a 3-course meal for one person.

£££ over £800Kč
££ 400Kč–£800Kč
£ under 400Kč

D6 Tomášská 12 257 532 344 Tram 12, 20, 22, 23 to Malostranské námestí

KAMPA FISH (££)

The Kolkovna Group's latest venture is this gastronomic fish and seafood restaurant, with a stylish interior and a riverside terrace.

E6 U Lužického semináře 42 257 531 799 Malostranská

KAMPA PARK (££–£££)

The place to come for celebrity spotting in a lovely riverside setting.

E7 Na Kampě 8b 296 826 102 Malostranská Tram 12, 22, 23 to Malostranské náměstí

PÁLFFY PALÁC (££–£££)

Offering serious cuisine in a comfortable atmosphere at prices that won't break the bank, this place has been popular among those in the know for years.

D6 Valdštejnksá 14 257 530 522 Malostranská

PETŘINSKÉ TERASY (£–££)

Enjoy well-prepared Czech specialties on the terrace or in the winter garden. Spectacular views.

C8 Seminářská zahrada 13 257 320 688 Tram 12, 20, 22, 23 to Hellichova, then walk or take the funicular uphill one stop

SOVOVY MLÝNY (££)

The restaurant attached to the modern art gallery in the beautifully restored 'Sova's Mill' offers innovative interpretations of traditional Bohemian dishes such as rabbit and goose. Outdoor dining on the riverside terrace.

E8 U Sovových Mlýnů, Kampa Island 257 535 900 Tram 12, 20, 22, 23 to Hellichova

FAST FOOD

Western fast food is now available in many places, but better by far (and much cheaper) for a quick snack are the local *obložené chlebíčky* (open-faced sandwiches). Each of these is like a miniature meal, perhaps consisting of a sliver or two of ham or salami and a slice of hard-boiled egg, the whole garnished with mayonnaise and topped with pieces of pickle and red pepper.

U KOCOURA (££–£££)

The famous old Tomcat is a welcome sight on the hard trek up from Malá Strana to Prague Castle.

D7 Nerudova 2 257 530 107 Tram 12, 20, 22, 23 to Malostranské náměstí

U MALÍŘŮ (£££)

Following a change of ownership, French-inspired cuisine continues to be served to a demanding clientele in a 16th-century building.

D7 Maltézské náměstí 11 257 530 318 Tram 12, 20, 22, 23 to Malostranské náměstí/ Hellichova

U MODRÉ KACHNIČKY (££)

The original nest of the 'Blue Duckling' is still going strong after having bred a twin in the Old Town. In its cosy side-street location it continues to serve delicious variations on venerable Czech dishes, particularly game.

D7 Nebovidská 6 257 320 308 Tram 12, 20, 22, 23 to Hellichova

Prague's suburbs and outer districts have much to offer. As well as musical shrines to Mozart and Dvořak there are historic buildings like Trojský zámek. The young-at-heart will enjoy the zoo.

DOLNÍ ŠÁRKA
Sárecky potok
Zoologická zahrada
Trojský zámek
BABA
240
Císařský ostrov
pruplav
HANSPAULKA
BUBENEČ
DEJVICE
EVROPSKA
7
OŘECHOVKA
MILADY HORÁKOVÉ
Letenské
VELESLAVÍN
HRADČANY
STŘEŠOVICE
Müllerova vila
STŘEŠOVICKY
PATOČKOVA
Břevnovský klášter
6
Lobkovická zahrada
MALÁ STRANA
STRAHOV
Strelecký ostrov
Petrinské sady
Slovanský ostrov
Kinského zahrada
Detský ostrov
PODBĚLOHORSKÁ
Klamovka
MOTOL
Vltava
Husovy sady
PLZEŇSKA
5
Bertramka
Sady na Skalce
Santoška
SMÍCHOV
Cibulka
KOŠÍŘE
Malvazinky
RADLICKÁ
RADLICE
4
JINONICE
ZLÍCHOV
0
1 km
0
1 mile
Zbraslav
HLUBOČEPY

608
TROJA
TROJSKA
PELC-TYRLOKA
V HOLEŠOVIČKÁCH
Letecké muzeum
VYCHOVATELNA
Vltava
LIBEŇ
Výstaviště
U URANIE
Thomayerovy sady
Stromovka
HOLEŠOVICE
Veletržní palác
LETNÁ
Národní technické muzeum
Vltava
KARLÍN
sady
Ostrov Štvanice
ROHANSKÉ NÁBŘEŽÍ
Kaizlovy sady
JOSEFOV
Vrch Vítkov
PRAGUE
Národní památník
STARÉ MĚSTO
ŽIŽKOV
Vrchlického sady
Olšanské hřbitovy
Riegrovy sady
Chram Nejsvětějšího Srdce Páně
VINOHRADY
VINOHRADSKA
ŽITNÁ
Sady Svat Čecha
NOVÉ MĚSTO
Bezrucovy sady
RUSKÁ
Heroldovy sady
Havlíčkovy sady
Folimanka
VRŠOVICKÁ
VYŠEHRAD
Vyšehradské sady
NUSELSKÁ
Botič
NA BOHDALCI
NUSLE
TYRŠŮV VRCH
Veslařský ostrov
PANKRÁC
MICHLE
PODOLÍ
Park Družby
DVORCE
KAČEROV
JEREMENKOVA

Trojský zámek

HIGHLIGHTS

- Garden approach on river side of château
- South staircase and terrace with battling Titans
- Grand Hall paintings

TIP

- A good idea is to combine a trip to Troja Château with a visit to Prague Zoo, badly hit by the great flood of 2002 but back in full working order, with a whole host of improvements.

Out here you catch a glimpse of how delightful Prague's countryside must have been three centuries ago, with vine-clad slopes, trees in abundance and the resplendent Troja Château among the allées and parterres.

Prague's Versailles This extravagant baroque palace was built not by the monarch, but by the second richest man in Prague, Count Wenceslas Adelbert Šternberg. The Šternbergs profited from the Thirty Years War, and at the end of the 17th century were in a position to commission Jean-Baptiste Mathey to design a country house along the lines of the contemporary châteaux of the architect's native France. The south-facing site by the river, orientated directly on St. Vitus's Cathedral and Prague

Clockwise from the left: the double staircase leading to the Troja Château; detail of relief decoration on a massive urn crowning a wall in the grounds of the château; wrought-iron gates at the entrance; the red and white façade of Troja château; the statue of a mermaid rising from the ornamental pond

Castle on the far side of the Royal Hunting Grounds, now Stromovka Park, was ideal for Šternberg, and it allowed him to offer the monarch the right kind of hospitality following a day's hunting.

Ornamental extravagance The palace's proportions are grandiose, and its painted interiors go over the top in paying homage to the country's Habsburg rulers. And over the top, too, goes a turbaned Turk as he topples, in stunning trompe l'oeil, from the mock battlements in the grand hall. Troja was acquired by the state in the 1920s, but restored only in the late 1980s (some think excessively). It contains part of Prague's collection of 19th-century paintings, few of which can compete with the flamboyance of their setting.

www.
citygalleryprague.cz

E1

U Trojského zámku 1, Troja

283 851 614

Tue–Sun 10–6

Restaurant

Nádraží Holešovice, then bus 112 to Zoologická zahrada

Trams 5, 12, 17 to Výstaviště, then walk across Stromovka Park and Císařský ostrov (Imperial Island) towards zoo

PPS boat from Palackého most, Nové Město

Few

Moderate

Veletržní palác

HIGHLIGHTS

- *Winter Evening in Town,* Jakub Schikaneder
- *Reader of Dostoyevsky,* Emil Filla
- *Serie C VI,* František Kupka
- *Melancholy,* Jan Zrzavý
- *Sailor,* Karel Dvořak

TIP

- Trying to see all the works on display in the Trade Fair Palace in one go is likely to lead to visual indigestion. Since tickets are available separately for the individual floors of the gallery, decide on your priorities and plan accordingly. If time is short, you might like to concentrate on the remarkable early-20th-century Czech art on the third floor.

'A truly great experience was a tour of the Prague Trade Fair Building. The first impression...is breathtaking'. So enthused architect Le Corbusier in 1928, shortly after this structure, now the Museum of Modern Art, was completed.

Trailblazer The great master builder and design pioneer Le Corbusier was vexed to find that his Czech colleagues had got in first in completing what is one of the key buildings in the evolution of 20th-century design, a secular, modern-day cathedral constructed in concrete, steel and glass. Set in the suburb of Holešovice, the palace was intended to be a showpiece for the products of Czechoslovakia. However, trade fairs moved away from Prague to Brno, and for many years the great building

Clockwise from the left: the exterior of Veletržní palác; the gallery displaying Czech art from 1930–2000; penny farthing bicycle with Contemplation *(1893) by Jakub Schikaneder in background;* Motorcyclist (sunbeam), *1924, by Otakar Svec; 1960s Skoda convertible display*

languished in neglect and obscurity, its originality forgotten as its architectural innovations became the norm throughout the world.

Disguised blessing After fire gutted the palace in 1974, it was decided to use its elegant spaces to display the National Gallery's modern art treasures, which had previously been without a proper home. The restoration took around 20 years. Now the engrossing Czech 19th-century collection leads the way to the amazing achievements of Czech artists in the early part of the 20th century. The museum also shows works by French Impressionists and other modern foreign paintings, and promotes contemporary arts of all types, staging the kind of major international art shows of which the Czechs were so long deprived.

THE BASICS

www.ngprague.cz
H4
Dukelských hrdinů 47, Holešovice
224 301 111
Tue–Sun 10–6
Café
Vltavská
Tram 5, 12, 14 from Náměstí Republiky to Veletržní
Good
Moderate (free first Wed of the month from 3pm)

Národní technické muzeum

An early car (left); a guided tour viewing some of the exhibits

THE BASICS

www.ntm.cz
G5
Kostelní 42, Holešovice
220 399 200
The museum is closed for reconstruction and is scheduled to reopen in 2008
Trams 1, 8, 18, 26 to Letenské náměstí, or Metro Vltavská then tram 1 to Letenské náměstí
Few
Moderate

HIGHLIGHTS

- 1928 Škoda fire engine
- Laurin and Klement soft-top roadster
- President Masaryk's V-12 Tatra
- Soviet ZIS 110B limousine
- Express locomotive 375-007 of 1911
- Imperial family's railway dining car of 1891
- Bleriot XI Kašpar monoplane
- Sokol monoplane

Did you know that Czechoslovakia had one of the world's biggest auto industries and that Škoda cars are legendary for their reliability? That a horse-drawn railway once linked Bohemia with Austria? That a Czechoslovak fleet once sailed the oceans?

Past glories The answer to all these questions will be 'yes', after you've visited the wonderful National Technical Museum, off the beaten track on the edge of Letenské sady (Letná Plain). The museum's rich and varied contents celebrate the longstanding technological prowess of inventive and hard-working Czechs. The Czech provinces were the industrial powerhouse of the Austro-Hungarian Empire, their steel works and coal mines providing the foundation for excellence in engineering, from the production of weapons to locomotive manufacture. Later, between the two world wars, independent Czechoslovakia's light industries led the world in innovation and quality.

Trains and boats and planes The museum's collection of technological objects is displayed to spectacular effect in the vast glass-roofed and galleried main hall, where balloons and biplanes hang in space above ranks of sinister-looking streamlined limousines and powerful steam engines. Deep underground there's a mock-up of a coal mine, and other sections tell you all you ever wanted to know about time, sound, geodesy, photography and astronomy.

More to See

BERTRAMKA

This villa was the rural retreat of the Dušeks, Mozart's closest friends in Prague, and it was here that he dashed off the final lines of *Don Giovanni* before conducting its premiere in the Estates Theatre. As well as Mozart memorabilia, on summer evenings, concerts take place in the park-like grounds.
C11 Mozartova 169, Smíchov 257 316 753 Daily 9–6 Tram 4, 7, 9, 10 to Bertramka Inexpensive

BŘEVNOSKÝ KLÁŠTER

The 1,000-year-old Benedictine monastery of Břevnov still has a rustic atmosphere. Its baroque buildings are the work of the Dientzenhofers, and include one of their grandest churches, and an array of other edifices.
Off map A7 Marketská 1/28, Řevnov, Prague 6 220 406 111 Apr–end Oct Sat, Sun 10am, 2pm, 4pm; Nov–end Mar Sat, Sun 10am, 2pm; guided tours only (in Czech) Inexpensive Tram 15, 22, 25 to Břevnovský klášter

CHRAM NEJSVĚTĚJŠÍHO SRDCE PÁNĚ

Completed in 1932 in Vinohrady, the modern Sacred Heart church is the masterwork of the Slovene Josip Plečnik, the architect employed in the interwar years to convert Prague Castle into a fitting symbol of the newly created democratic state of Czechoslovakia.
Off map J9 Náměstí Jiřího z Poděbrad 19, Vinohrady 222 727 713 30 min before and 1 hour after services. Sun 9, 11, 6; Mon–Sat 8–6 Jiřího z Poděbrad

LETECKE MUZEUM

This has one of Europe's largest collections of historic aircraft. Interwar machines demonstrate the vigour of the Czechoslovak aircraft industry then. But the stars of the show are the World War II aircraft.
Off map J1 Mladoboleslavská 902, Kbely 973 207 500 Apr–Oct Tue–Sun 10–6 Českomoravská, then bus 259, 280, 302, 349, 354, 375, 376 to Letecké Muzeum Free

The temple-like structure of the Sacred Heart Church

The interior vaults of the Benedictine Monastery of Brevnov

MÜLLEROVA VILA

www.mullerovavila.cz

The villa, built for the Müller family in 1930, is a key building in the evolution of Functionalist architecture. Its designer was the Viennese architect Adolf Loos (1870–1933). The exterior is severe, but the spatial austerity of the interior is relieved by the use of precious materials.

A6 · Nad Hradním vodojemem 14, Střešovice, Prague 6 · 224 312 012 · Guided tours Tue, Thu, Sat, Sun at 9, 11, 1, 3, 5. Tours must be booked ahead · Expensive · Hradčanská, then tram · Tram 1, 2, 18 to Ořechovka

NÁRODNÍ PAMÁTNÍK (NATIONAL MEMORIAL)

Built to commemorate the Czechoslovak legions that fought on the Allied side in World War I, this great slab of a building overlooking the city features a huge equestrian statue of the Hussite, Jan Žižka.

Off map J7 · U Památníku 1900 · 222 781 676 · Guided tours by prior arrangement (groups of more than 20) · Bus 133, 207 to U Památníku and steep uphill walk

VÝSTAVIŠTĚ

The extensive Exhibition Grounds offer an array of attractions, including a fun fair, performance spaces and a spectacular fountain. Nearby is the Planetarium.

G/H3 · U Výstaviště, Holešovice · 220 103 111 · Tue–Fri from 2pm, Sat, Sun from 10am (evening opening for performances) · Cafés and restaurants · Tram 5, 12, 14, 17 to Výstaviště · Inexpensive

ZBRASLAV

Visitors come here to see the Zbraslavský zámek, the baroque palace, which is home to the National Gallery's collections of Oriental art and objects.

Off map E12 · Bartoňova 2, Zbraslav, Prague 5 · 257 921 638 · Tue–Sun 10–6 · Inexpensive · Bus 129, 241, 243, 255, 360 from Smíchovské nádraží metro station to Zbraslavské náměstí (14 min)

Tomb guardians, Western Jin dynasty, c.300BC, in the Zbraslavský zámek in the town of Zbraslav

Prumyslový palác in Výstaviště (Exhibition Park)

Excursions

HRAD KARLŠTEJN (KARLŠTEJN CASTLE)

This mighty fortress, one of the great sights of Bohemia, towers above the glorious woodlands of the gorge of the River Berounka. The castle was started in 1348 by the Emperor Charles IV who conceived it as a sort of sacred bunker, a repository for the Crown Jewels and his collection of holy relics.

THE BASICS

www.hradkarlstejn.cz
Distance 35km (21 miles)
Journey Time 40 mins
☎ Reservations: 274 008 154; castle 311 681 617
🚆 Prague–Smíchov to Karlštejn

ZÁMEK KONOPIŠTĚ (KONOPIŠTĚ CASTLE)

Konopiště Castle's round towers rise in romantic fashion above the surrounding woodlands. The palace's origins date to the 14th century, but it owes its present appearance largely to Archduke Franz Ferdinand, heir to the Habsburg throne, who filled it with trophies of the countless wild creatures he slaughtered. The archduke met his own violent end when he was cut down by an assassin's bullet in Sarajevo, triggering the start of World War I. The castle is full of Franz Ferdinand's fine furniture and his collection of weapons.

THE BASICS

www.zamek-konopiste.cz
Distance 43km (26 miles)
Journey Time 45 mins by car; 1 hour by train then short distance by local bus or taxi
☎ 17 721 336 🕓 Check locally or on website
🚆 Train to Benešov from Hlavní nádraží (1 hour) then bus or taxi

KUTNA HORA

One of Bohemia's best-preserved old towns has abundant relics from the glory days when it was a great silver mining hub. A stroll around the streets leads past many minor treasures, such as the Gothic Kamenný dům (Stone House) and the venerable 12-sided public fountain. The town's finest monument is the great Chrám svaté Barbory (St. Barbara's Church), a cathedral-size structure, one of Europe's most extraordinary achievements of late Gothic architecture. In the suburb of Sedlec is a macabre item, the bones from some 40,000 burials in a vaulted ossuary.

THE BASICS

Tourist information office
www.kutnohorsko.cz
Distance 70km (43 miles)
Journey Time 1 hour 15 minutes by bus from Florenc bus station

✉ Sankturinovský dům , Palackého náměstí, 284 01 Kutná Hora
☎ 327 512 378

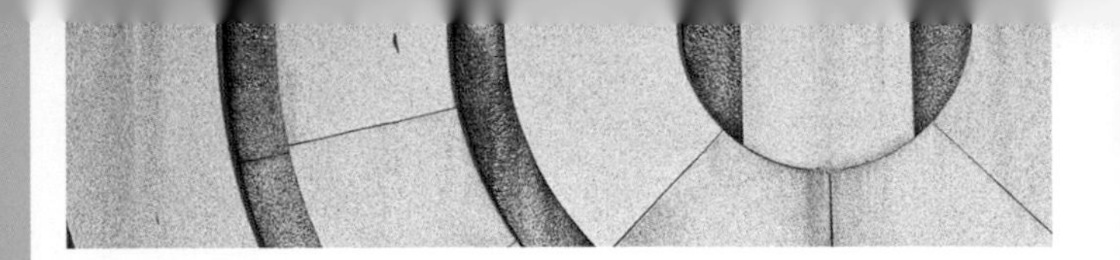

THE BASICS

General information
Distance 27km (17 miles)
Journey time Local train to Nelahozeves zastávka (50 min)

Zámek Nelahozeves
www.lobkowiczevents.cz
✉ 277 51 Nelahozeves
🕐 Tue–Sun 9–12, 1–4 (guided tour)

Památník Antonín Dvořáka
www.nm.cz
✉ 27751 Nelahozeves
🕐 1st and 3rd week in month, Wed–Sun 9.30–12, 1–5; 2nd and 4th week in month, Wed–Fri 9.30–12, 1–5

NELAHOZEVES

This otherwise unpretentious village on the banks of the Vltava north of Prague has two major attractions, the birthplace of composer Antonín Dvořák, and a magnificent château. Dvořák's humble home has plenty of memorabilia, while the castle, a splendid example of Italian-inspired Bohemian Renaissance architecture, is a treasure house of art, with one of Europe's outstanding private painting collections. Among the pictures restituted to the owners, the princely Lobkowicz family, is *Haymaking* by Pieter Brueghel the Elder, once the pride of Prague's National Gallery. The building itself, approached via a bridge across a dry moat, has three completed wings, on the courtyard, in different styles. Although the interior is now mostly visited for the collections, there are many fascinating areas, particularly the Arkádové haly (Arcade Hall) and the vaulted Rytířský sál (Knights Hall).

THE BASICS

Distance 65km (40 miles)
Journey time Around 1 hour from Florenc bus station

General information
Terezín–Památník (Terezín–Memorial
Principova alej 304, 411 55 Terezín
www.pamatnik-terezin.cz
☎ 416 782 225/416 782 442

TEREZIN

In World War II, the Nazis cleared this 18th-century barrack town of its inhabitants and turned it into a ghetto for Czechoslovak and German Jews. Deceitfully portraying it as a model community, they succeeded in fooling the International Red Cross, but in reality Terezín was simply a staging post for the Final Solution, and most of those incarcerated here met their end in Auschwitz. The Muzeum Ghetta (Ghetto Museum) tells the place's awful story. Outside the walls is the Malá pevnost (Small Fortress), originally an Austrian political prison, then a far more horrible jail for Gestapo victims of many nationalities.

Where to Stay

Like all major cities, Prague has a range of accommodation, from sleek, modern hotels and magnificent converted old buildings to hostels and cottages.

Introduction

Prague offers an extraordinary range of places to stay in almost every category, with a distinct emphasis on hotels in historic buildings.

You can stay in grand old buildings when you visit Prague

New hotels

A building boom has created an impressive increase in the number of four- and five-star establishments. Nevertheless, official room rates remain high, though you should always check whatever special offers are available. Prague is an all-seasons city, and it is prudent to book well in advance, at any time of the year.

Practical considerations

The location of your accommodation is crucial. Efficient public transport may get you quickly from your suburban hotel to the city, but since Prague is such a delight to explore on foot, you may want to look for lodgings in one of the historic quarters within walking distance of some of the main attractions. Room rates are often quoted in euros as well as Czech crowns. Credit cards are widely accepted.

Longer stays

If your stay is more than a few days, it could be well worthwhile renting an apartment or even a room in a private flat. Some of the former are in outstanding settings, with, for example, river views, while private rooms tend to be out in the suburbs.

ACCOMMODATION ADVICE

One of the most reliable kiosks at the main station is that of the Prague Information Service (P.I.S), who also can arrange accommodation at their other information offices. P.I.S also offer online reservation through their accommodation agency Pragotur ✉ Arbesovo náměstí 4, Prague 5 ☎ 221 714 130. E-mail: pragotur@pis.cz.

A reliable private agency is Stop City ✉ Vinohradská 24, Vinohrady ☎ 222 251 233/4.

Budget Hotels

PRICES

Between 1,850Kč and £2,700Kč per night for a budget hotel.

ATLANTIC

www.hotel-atlantic.cz

Refurbished accommodation near the Municipal House in a medium size establishment, which is a member of the Small Charming Hotels group.

H6 Na Poříčí 9, eastern New Town 224 811 084 Náměstí Republiky

BÍLÝ LEV

A good-value, 27-room place in the funky eastern suburb of Žižkov.

Off map J7 Cimburkova 20 222 780 430; fax 222 780 465 Trams 5, 9, 26 to Husinecká

KAFKA

Good-value, 50-room hotel on the wrong side of the tracks in Žižkov, but only 10 minutes' walk from the main train station.

G4 Cimburkova 24 222 781 333 Tram 5, 9, 26 to Husinecká

LUNÍK

www.hotel-lunik-cz

Special offers can bring this comfortable, family-style small hotel into the easily affordable category. It's just a few steps from the nearest metro station and an easy walk to the top of Wenceslas Square.

H9 Londýnská 50, Vinohrady 224 253 974 Náměstí Míru

MARKÉTA

www.europehotels.cz

Bright, cheery 26-room hotel in a quiet street in the pleasant suburbs to the west of the Castle.

Off map A7 Na Petynce 45, Břevnov 220 518 316 Hradčanská, then bus 108, 174 to Katjetánk

SALVATOR

www.salvator.cz

Friendly, 32-room courtyard hotel, very near the Municipal House.

H6 Truhlářská 10, Nové Město 222 312 234 Náměstí Republiky

TARA

www.pensiontara.net

Straightforward accommodation in a tiny eight-room pension that overlooks the Havelská street market in the heart of the Old Town. Rooms are on the third and fourth floors and that there is no elevator.

F7 Havelská 15, Staré Město 224 228 108 Můstek

HOSTELS

A number of hostels stand ready to look after the swarms of backpackers passing through Prague on their travels. A popular one offering single rooms as well as dorms and with several branches in the city and elsewhere is: Traveller's Hostel www.travellers.cz

G6 Dlouhá 33, Old Town 224 826 662 Náměstí Republiky

TOSCA

www.hotel-tosca.cz

Modestly furnished but comfortable accommodation just around the corner from a metro station and within walking distance of Wenceslas Square.

J10 Blanická 10, Vinohrady 221 506 111 Náměstí Míru

TŘÍSKA

www.hoteltriska.cz

A friendly place on the main drag through Vinohrady. Each of the individually furnished rooms has a refrigerator. No credit cards.

Off map J9 Vinhohradská 105 222 727 313 Jiřího z Poděbrad

U ŠUTERŮ

www.usuteru.cz

Ten-room establishment in an historic building in a side street just a few steps from Wenceslas Square. Astonishing value for such a location plus a characterful restaurant on the ground floor.

G8 Palackého 4, New Town 224 948 235 Můstek

Mid-Range Hotels

PRICES

Between 2,700Kč and 5,200Kč per night for a mid-range hotel.

AMETYST

www.hotelametyst.cz

A fresh and inviting 84-room, family-owned hotel, the equal in luxury to most of the big names and only 10 minutes' walk from Wenceslas Square.

J10 Jana Masaryka 11, Vinohrady 222 921 921 Náměstí Míru

ANNA

www.hotelanna.cz

A reliable 23-room hotel in the pleasant inner suburb of Vinohrady, less than 15 minutes' stroll from Wenceslas Square.

Off map J10 Budečská 17, Vinohrady 222 513 111 Náměstí Míru

BETLEM CLUB

www.betlemclub.cz

A small 22-room hotel offering accommodation in the same square as Jan Hus's historic Bethlehem Chapel.

F8 Betlémské náměstí 9, Staré Město 222 221 574 Národní třída

CENTRAL

www.orfea.cz

Somewhat sparse but quite adequate, the Central is located behind the Municipal House, with 68 rooms.

G7 Rybná 8, Staré Město 224 812 041 Náměstí Republiky

CLOISTER INN

www.cloister-inn.com

Adequate 75-room hotel between the National Theatre and the Bethlehem Chapel.

F8 Konviktská 14, Staré Město 224 211 020 Národní třída

HAŠTAL

www.hastal.com

A simple 24-room hotel, in a former brewery. Nice views over a quiet square.

G6 Haštalská 16, Staré Město 222 314 335 Tram 5, 14, 26 to louhá třída

HOTEL 16 U SV KATEŘINY

www.hotel16.cz

Excellent-value family hotel, with 14 rooms. Close to the Dvořák Museum and the botanical gardens, and 10 minutes' walk from Wenceslas Square.

G10 Kateřinská 16, Nové Město 224 920 636 I P Pavlova

BOTELS

An alternative to conventional hotels are the 'botels' moored at various points along the banks of the Vltava. However, being rather cramped, they are less romantic than they might sound. One such, close to the Palacký Bridge (Palackého most) on the Smíchov quayside, is the Admirál (257 321 302).

IBIS

www.accorhotels.com

The Accor group has several hotels in Prague, among them four bearing the Ibis name, all of which offer reliable, predictable accommodation and facilities. Of the four, the most centrally located is the newly opened Ibis Praha Old Town; the claimed location is something of an exaggeration since it is actually in the eastern part of the New Town, albeit literally just a few steps from the Municipal House.

H7 (Ibis Praha Old Town) Na Poříčí 7, eastern New Town 221 800 800 Náměstí Republiky

LUNIK

www.hotel-lunik.cz

Attractive 1920s ambience in a small hotel within easy reach of the upper end of Wenceslas Square.

H9 Londýnská 50, Vinohrady 224 263 974 Tram 5, 14, 26 to Náměstí Míru

MAXIMILIAN

www.maximilianhotel.com

The historic 1904 building has been beautifully reconstructed in art nouveau style with

attention to every detail. G6 Haštalská 14, Staré Město 225 303 118 Tram 5, 14, 26 to Dlouhá třída

MÖVENPICK

www.moevenpick-prague.com

High standard of comfort and facilities in the Smíchov branch of this chain, whose buildings are spectacularly linked by funicular. With 436 rooms.

C11 Mozartova 261/1 257 151 111 Anděl

NOVOMĚSTSKÝ HOTEL

www.novomestskyhotel.cz

A small hotel on a quiet street by the New Town Hall, with a high standard for the lowish room rates.

G9 Řeznická 4, Nové Město 222 231 498 Karlovo náměstí

SAX

www.sax.cz

This 22-room hotel just off Nerudova Street offers views of Malá Strana.

C7 Janský vršek 3 257 531 268 Tram 12, 22, 23 to Malostranské náměstí then an uphill walk

SIEBER

www.sieber.cz

This gracious family-run establishment offers 20 luxurious rooms and suites. A giant step up from the average mid-range hotel.

Off map J9 Slezská 55, Vinohrady 224 250 025 Jiřího z Poděbrad Tram 10, 16 to Perunova

TCHAIKOVSKY

www.hoteltchaikovsky.com

A tasteful 19-room hotel near Karlovo náměstí, the Dvořák museum and the botanical gardens.

G10 Ke Karlovu 19, Nové Město 224 912 121 Karlovo náměstí/ I.P. Pavlova

U KRÁLE JIŘÍHO

www.kinggeorge.cz

A small hotel just off the Royal Way with 17 comfortable rooms and the dubious bonus of a pub on the ground floor.

F7 Liliová 10, Staré Město 221 466 100 Staroměstská

COUNTRY COTTAGE

In days gone by, many of the houses on the outskirts of the city were built of timber in log cabin style. The only one remaining is U Raka (the 'House at the sign of the Crayfish'), in the tranquil surroundings of Nový Svět in the Castle quarter. It has been turned into an exquisite little hotel, beautifully fitted out in rustic style, with just a few bedrooms. www.romantikhotel-uraka.cz

B6 Černínská 10, Hradčany 220 511 100 Tram 22, 23 to Brusnice

U KRÁLE KARLA

Nestling at the foot of steps leading up to Hradčany Square, the comfortable King Charles exudes historic atmosphere, unsurprisingly, since the building it occupies goes back to the Middle Ages. Note that it's an uphill walk from the tram stop.

C7 257 532 869 Tram to Malostranské náměstí

U LILIE

www.pensionulilie.cz

This 17-room pension is in a medieval house close to Charles Bridge.

F7 Liliová 15, Staré Město 222 220 432 Staroměstská

U MEDVÍDKŮ

www.umedvidku.cz

The 33-room pension features beautiful beamed ceilings. The famous pub of the same name is downstairs.

F8 Na Perštýne 7, Staré Město 224 211 916 Národní třída

UNION

www.hotelunion.cz

A 57-room art nouveau hotel with comfortable and stylish rooms set in a quiet square.

G12 Ostrčilovo náměstí 4, Nusle 261 214 812 Tram 18, 24 to Ostrčilovo náměstí

Luxury Hotels

PRICES

Expect to pay upwards of 5,200Kč per night for a luxury hotel.

ADRIA

www.adria.cz

This is a stunningly restored 87-room hotel set amid the bustle of Wenceslas Square.

Václavské náměstí 26 221 081 111 Můstek

ARIA

www.aria.cz

An exquisite and very original 52-room hotel, designed and run on the theme of music.

D7 Tržiště 9, Malá Strana 225 334 111 Tram 12, 20, 22, 23 to Malostranské náměstí

BOSCOLO CARLO IV

www.boscolohotels.com

This magnificent neo-classical palace on a square between the main station and the Municipal House is now one of Prague's most sumptuous hotels.

H7 Senovážné náměstí 13 224 593 111 Hlavní nadráží/Náměstí Republiky

FOUR SEASONS HOTEL PRAGUE

Supremely luxurious conversion of a group of historic buildings near Charles Bridge.

F7 Veleslavínova 2a, Staré Město 221 427 000 Staroměstská

INTERCONTINENTAL

www.prague.intercontinental.com

This 364-room hotel was the epitome of pretension when it opened in the 1970s. Near Josefov, it has every comfort, as well as large public rooms furnished with antiques.

F6 Náměstí Curieových 5 296 631 111 Staroměstská

IRON GATE HOTEL & SUITES

www.irongate.cz

Luxury in a beautifully adapted 14th-century courtyard building in a cobbled street near Old Town Square.

F7 Michalská 19, Old Town 225 777 777 Staroměstská/Můstek

JOSEF

www.hoteljosef.com

This design hotel features 110 rooms of cool luxury and every conceivable amenity.

G6 Rybná 20, Staré Město 221 700 111 Náměstí Republiky

OFFERS

The number of visitors to Prague has tended to stabilize, while provision of luxury accommodation has expanded rapidly. The rack rates charged by luxury hotels are as high as anywhere in the world, but most will offer substantial discounts at slack periods. It's worth checking whether such offers are available while planning your trip.

K&K CENTRAL

www.kkhotels.com

The equal in terms of opulent art nouveau architecture to the famous Evropa, the Central easily outclasses its rival in its comfort, convenience and inventive adaptation.

H7 Hybernská 10, northern New Town 225 022 000 Náměstí Republiky

MANDARIN ORIENTAL

www.mandarinoriental.com

This new luxury hotel is a conversion of a 14th-century monastery in Malá Strana. In an adjoining, equally venerable building, is the Spa, with a whole range of tempting treatments.

D7 Nebovidská 1, Malá Strana 233 088 888 Tram 12, 20, 22, 23 to Hellichova

YASMIN

www.hotel-yasmin.cz

A significant addition to Prague's range of designer hotels, Yasmin upstages most of its rivals in sheer verve and trendiness. There's a Summer Garden and a Noodle Café and Bar.

H7 Politickýh vězňů 12, New Town 234 100 100 Muzeum/Můstek

Need to Know

Use this section to help you plan your visit to Prague. We have suggested the best ways to get around the city and useful information for when you are there.

Planning Ahead

When to Go

The best times to visit are in spring, when the fruit trees of Petřín Hill are in blossom, and in early summer, before the throngs of tourists arrive. Most tourists visit between May and September. Christmas and New Year see the main squares become decorated markets and later rowdy New Year's Eve party sites.

TIME

Prague is one hour ahead of the UK, six hours ahead of New York and nine hours ahead of Los Angeles.

AVERAGE DAILY MAXIMUM TEMPERATURES

JAN	FEB	MAR	APR	MAY	JUN	JUL	AUG	SEP	OCT	NOV	DEC
30°F	32°F	39°F	48°F	57°F	63°F	66°F	64°F	57°F	48°F	39°F	32°F
-1°C	0°C	4°C	9°C	14°C	17°C	19°C	18°C	14°C	9°C	4°C	0°C

Spring (March–May) starts out cold and damp but turns beautiful in April and May, with blooming trees and gardens throughout the city.
Summer (June–August) can be oppressively hot and humid, with heavy rainfall.
Autumn (September–November) is a lovely time, with bright, sunny days through October and dwindling numbers of tourists. The weather has cooled considerably by November.
Winter (December–February) can be depressingly grey and cold, with high levels of air pollution.

WHAT'S ON

April/May *Agharta Prague Jazz Festival*: Going strong since 1992, this festival (www.agharta.cz) brings in jazz and blues acts from all over the world. It is sponsored by the Agharta jazz club and is held in venues throughout the city.
May *Prague Spring Music Festival* (mid-May): This international event (www.festival.cz) consists of an array of classical music concerts which are held in churches, palaces and halls throughout the city. It starts with a procession from Smetana's grave in the National Cemetery in Vyšehrad to the great hall named after him in the restored Obecní dům (Municipal House), where a rousing performance of his orchestral tone poem *Má Vlast* (My Country) is given.
June *Dance Prague*: Dance festival with events at various venues, including outdoor spaces.
July/August Summer festivals of early music (www.tynska.cuni.cz).
December *St. Nicholas* (5 December): A multitude of St. Nicks roam the streets, accompanied by an angel who rewards good children with candy and a devil who chastizes appropriately.
Christmas Eve (24 December): Live carp are sold on the streets for the traditional Czech Christmas Eve dinner.
New Year's Eve (31 December): There are formal Sylvester balls and, outside, crowds welcome the arrival of the New Year on the streets.

Prague Online

www.prague-info.cz
Information on museums, monuments, cultural schedules and Prague history, along with tips, accommodation and general tourist listings from Prague's official information service.

www.czechtourism.com
Czech Tourism's website provides information on agrotourism, UNESCO-graded monuments, cycling, mountaineering and other outdoor activities, along with useful practical planning information.

www.prague-tourist-information.com
Includes comprehensive advice on transport, tourist tips, sightseeing, museums, a restaurant guide and a section on children's Prague.

www.radio.cz
News, history, interesting features and information on upcoming events from Radio Prague.

www.czech.cz
The Foreign Ministry's site has specifics on travelling, studying and doing business in the Czech Republic.

www.prague2001.com
Plenty of useful tips for your trip to Prague plus good coverage on nightlife.

www.praguepost.com
The online version of the city's weekly English-language paper, with news, comprehensive listings, and some visitor information.

www.prague.tv
City guide with accommodation finder, expat gossip and survival tips.

USEFUL TRAVEL SITE

www.fodors.com
A complete travel-planning site. You can research prices and weather; book air tickets, cars and rooms; pose questions to fellow travellers; and find links to other sites.

CYBERCAFÉS

Planeta
The city's best-value internet café.
H5 Vinohradská 102, Vinohrady 267 311 182; www.planeta.cz
0.40–0.60Kč per minute
Jiřího z Poděbřad

The Globe
Coffee, food and books. Plug-ins for laptops.
E5 Pštrossova 6, Nové Město 224 934 203; www.globebookstore.cz 1.5Kč per minute
Národní třída

Kava Kava Kava
Voted 'best coffee' in Prague.
D–E5 Národní 37 (in the Platýz courtyard), Staré Město 224 228 862; www.kava-coffee.cz
1.5–2Kč per minute
Nádrodní třída

Getting There

ENTRY REQUIREMENTS

Tourists from the UK, US and most European countries do not need visas. Be sure to check the latest requirements before travelling as they can change. Canadian visitors may require a visa.

DRIVING

- Road regulations are much the same in the Czech Republic as in the rest of Europe. They are rigorously enforced, with no allowances made for drivers from abroad.

- Speed limits in built-up areas (indicated by place-name signs) are 50kph (31mph). Outside built-up areas the limit is 90kph (56mph) and on motorways it is 130kph (80mph).

- A vignette (sticker) permitting the use of motorways must be purchased and displayed.

- Headlights must be on between November and March.

- Trams must be given priority.

- First-aid kit, warning triangle and spare light bulbs must be carried.

AIRPORTS

Ruzyně Airport is 17km (10 miles) northwest of downtown Prague and is served by direct flights from most major European cities, as well as New York and Montreal. There are shops, bars and a cafeteria. The national airline is ČSA (head office: ✉ V Celnící 5, Nové Město ☎ 239 007 007).

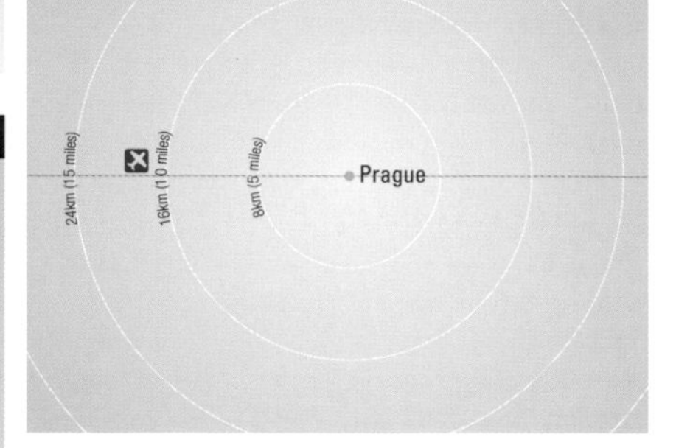

ARRIVING BY AIR

Airport information ☎ 220 111 111 (www.prg.aero). The most straightforward link from Ruzyně Airport to downtown is by minibus to Náměstí Republiky, on the eastern edge of the Old Town. The bus runs every half hour 5.30am–9.30pm. Pay at the Cedaz desk in the arrivals hall and pick up the white minibus in front of the terminal. The trip takes 20–30 minutes and costs Kč90 each way, bags included. City bus 119 goes to Dejvická metro station, from where it is only a few stops to downtown. Pick it up at the bus stand in front of the airport. Buy a Kč20 ticket inside at the DPP (Prague Transit Authority) office. Buses run 5am—midnight (journey time 20 mins). Bus 100 runs to Zličín metro station, which may be more convenient for western areas. Taxis can be picked up at the airport, but agree on the approximate fare beforehand. The cost is around Kč500 and the journey takes 25–45 minutes.

ARRIVING BY BUS

Express buses link Prague with international

destinations, including London. The main coach terminal is at Florenc, on the eastern edge of downtown, where there is also a metro station. You can buy tickets at the coach terminal in Florenc but it is easier to use a travel agent.

ARRIVING BY CAR

Good main roads link Prague to all adjoining countries, and the city is now linked by motorway D5/E50 to the German autobahn network via Plzeň and the Bavarian border. The D8/E55 motorway towards Dresden and Berlin is almost complete. Prague is 1,100km (683 miles) from Calais (France), with its ferry services to Dover (UK) as well as the Channel Tunnel Shuttle. Once in Prague a car is likely to be more of a hindrance than a help.

ARRIVING BY TRAIN

Express trains connect Prague to all adjoining countries. The most convenient rail route from London is by Eurostar to Brussels, then German railways overnight trains via Frankfurt or Berlin. Most trains terminate at Hlavní nádraží (Main Station F4), though some stop (or terminate) at Holešovice in the northern suburbs or at Smíchov in the southern suburbs, both of which have good metro connections. Czech Railways (ČD) has information offices in Main Station at the north end of level 3 (domestic) and the south end of the lower hall (international) ☎ 221 111 122 (www.vlak.cz).

INSURANCE

All visitors should have full tmedical and travel insurance. UK citizens may enjoy free medical treatment in an emergency, but taking out medical insurance ensures rapid repatriation and can help in cutting through bureaucracy.

DRIVING

- To drive on Czech motorways you need a toll sticker, which can be bought at the border or at post offices or fuel stations (Kč200 for 15 days; Kč300 for two months).
- Check that your insurance policy covers you to drive in the Czech Republic.
- The drink-drive limit is zero alcohol.
- No special licence is needed for tourists who stay less than 90 days.
- The map *Praha pro motoristy* (Prague for motorists) is an invaluable aid to driving in the city.

Getting Around

NATIONAL HOLIDAYS

1 January, Easter Monday, 1 May (Labour Day), 8 May (Liberation Day), 5 July (SS Cyril and Methodius), 6 July (Jan Hus's Day), 28 September (St. Wenceslas's Day), 28 October (Independence Day), 17 November (Day of Students), 24–26 December.

TELEPHONES

- With the exception of emergency numbers, taxi dispatchers and the like, only 9-digit numbers are valid. If in doubt, call directory inquiries ☎ 1180.
- Most public phones now take phone cards, on sale in kiosks and post offices. Telephoning from your hotel may cost four times the standard rate.
- To call the Czech Republic from the UK, dial 00 420. To call the UK from Prague, dial 00 44, then drop the first zero from the area code.
- To call the Czech Republic from the US, dial 00420. To call the US from Prague, dial 001.

PUBLIC TRANSPORT

- Public transport maps are available from the information offices at the airport and metro stations Muzeum, Můstek, Anděl, Černý Most and Nádraží Holešovice.
- Expect crowding during the rush hours (generally 7am–10am, 3pm–6pm). The young and fit should give up their seats to passengers who need them more.
- Valid for all forms of transport, tickets cost Kč14 (short trips) or Kč20 (valid 1–1.5 hours) and allow as many changes as necessary. They must be validated in the machines provided before your journey. One or three-day passes are available.

BUS

- Kept out of downtown to minimize pollution, buses serve all the suburban areas that the trams do not reach.

FUNICULAR

- The *lanovka* (funicular railway) climbs to the top of Petřin Hill from its Újezd station in Malá Strana via a halfway station at Nebozízek.
- You can use the normal public transport ticket.

METRO

- This showpiece system, with its fast and frequent trains and clean stations, consists of three lines: A (coded green), B (yellow) and C (red). They converge from the suburbs onto downtown, where there are several interchange stations.
- To get on the right train, check the line (A, B or C) and note the name of the terminus station at the end of the line in the direction you wish to travel; this station appears on the overhead direction signs.
- Outlying stations are relatively far apart and are intended to feed commuters to connecting trams and buses.
- Particularly useful stations are Můstek (for

Wenceslas Square and Old Town Square), Staroměstská (for Old Town Square) and Malostranská (for Malá Strana and for trams 22 and 23). Hradčanská station is 15 minutes' walk from Prague Castle.

TAXI

- Prague taxi drivers have a reputation for overcharging.
- Agree on the approximate fare beforehand. Ask for a receipt to reduce excessive demands.
- You may receive a more reliable service if you phone for a taxi or flag down a moving taxi rather than going to a taxi rank in a tourist area, where drivers have the worst reputation.
- For taxis, telephone AAA Radiotaxi ☎ 221 102 211 or Profitaxi ☎ 844 700 800.
- Smart hotels have their own taxi service, reliable but expensive.

TRAM

- The tramway system operates in close conjunction with the metro.
- The name of every tram stop appears on the stop sign and on the route map.
- Tram routes are numbered, and the tram has a destination board. Timetables are posted on the stop and are almost always adhered to.
- There is a skeleton service of night trams, with its own system of numbers and schedules.
- A particularly useful and scenic line is the No. 22/23, which runs from the city centre (at Národní třída) right through Malá Strana, past Malostranská metro station, then climbs to the back of Prague Castle (Pražský hrad stop) and continues to Strahov Monastery (Pohořelec stop).
- On weekends between April and November a veteran tram (Route No. 91) trundles along the tracks. It's a fun way of seeing the city.

MONEY

- There are plenty of cash machines in Prague, including at the airport, and instructions are usually in English as well as Czech.

- Children, students and older people are entitled to discounts for many services and attractions, though you might need to prove eligibility (passport or student card).

VISITORS WITH DISABILITIES

Many of the things that make Prague an enchanting city—cobblestoned streets Gothic towers with breathtaking views and red trams—can be notoriously difficult for visitors with disabilities to negotiate. The metro, too, has limited access; check which stations have facilities first. The website of the local organization Pražská organizace cozíčkářů (PUV) has comprehensive lists (in Czech) of accessible buildings (www.pov.cz).

Essential Facts

BE UP-TO-DATE

It is advisable to check visa and customs regulations before you travel as these can change at short notice.

MONEY

The Czech crown (*koruna česká* or Kč) is divided into 100 virtually worthless hellers (*haléř*). There are coins for 50 hellers, and for 1, 2, 5, 10, 20 and 50 crowns, and notes in denominations of 20, 50, 100, 200, 500, 1,000, 2,000 and 5,000 crowns.

20 Koruna

50 Koruna

100 Koruna

200 Koruna

CUSTOMS REGULATIONS

- The guidelines for EU residents (for personal use) are 800 cigarettes, 200 cigars, 1kg tobacco; 10 litres of spirits (over 22 percent), 20 litres of aperitifs, 90 litres of wine (60 can be sparkling wine), 110 litres of beer.
- The limits for non-EU visitors are 200 cigarettes or 100 cigars or 250g tobacco; 2 litres of wine; 1 litre of spirits; and personal items totalling 6,000Kč in value.
- Antiques and 'rare cultural objects' require an official certificate from a recognized museum or art gallery (which the dealer may already have obtained) when being exported from the Czech Republic.

ELECTRICITY

- 230 volts, 50 cycles AC, fed through standard Continental two-pin plugs.

ETIQUETTE

- Czech manners tend to be formal. Titles such as Doctor must not be ignored, and hands should be shaken when offered.
- Dress is less formal than it was. Neat casual wear is acceptable in most restaurants and tourist theatres. Smart dress is expected in other theatres and at the opera.
- Diners share tables in busy eateries and exchange greetings: *dobrý den* (good day) and *dobrou chuť* (enjoy your meal).
- Czechs invariably say *dobrý den* (hello) and *na shledanou* (goodbye) when entering or leaving an establishment.
- If you are invited to a Czech home, take flowers or a gift and remove your shoes at the door.

MONEY MATTERS

- There are bureaux de change, but banks and ATMs often give better exchange rates.
- Credit cards are in increasing use.

OPENING HOURS

- Banks: Mon–Fri 8–5.

● Shops: many downtown shops stay open until late weekdays and are also open weekends. In the suburbs and elsewhere, shops are open Mon–Fri 9–6, Sat 9–1.
● Museums and galleries: Tue–Sun 9/10–5. Most close Mon, except the National Museum and Prague Castle (open daily); the Jewish Museum is open Sun–Fri. Some museums also close for lunch.

PLACES OF WORSHIP
● Roman Catholic: sv Tomáše (St. Thomas's Church) ✉ Josefská 8, Malá Strana 🚇 Malostranská 🕐 English Mass Sun 11am
● Anglican: sv Klimenta (St. Clement's Church) ✉ Klimentská, Nové Město 🚇 Náměstí Republiky 🕐 English-language service Sun 11am
● Jewish: Staronová synagóga (Old/New Synagogue, ▷ 26–27) ✉ Pařížská and Červená 🚇 Staroměstská 🕐 Services Mon–Thu 8am, Fri sunset, Sat 9am

STUDENT VISITORS
● Few discounts are available for students, but keeping out of the most popular tourist spots makes Prague an affordable city.
● All aspects of youth travel are dealt with by the Student Agency ✉ Ječná 377, Nové Město ☎ 224 999 666 🚇 I P Pavlova

TOILETS
● 'WC', 'muži/páni' (Men) and 'ženy/dámy' (Women) are useful signs to remember.
● Public facilities are rare; look in restaurants, cafés, metro stations, etc.
● Tip the attendant with some smaller coins.

LOST PROPERTY

The office is at ✉ Karoliny Světlé 5, Staré Město ☎ 224 235 085

MEDICAL TREATMENT

Visitors from EU countries, including Britain, are entitled to free emergency medical treatment, though a charge may be made for medicines. Make sure you have your blue European Health Insurance Card with you. Private medical insurance is necessary for citizens of other countries, and is still advised for EU citizens. Your hotel reception will help direct you to appropriate treatment facilities. Hospitals and clinics used to dealing with foreigners include:

Nemocnice Na Homolce (public hospital)
✚ Off map A9
✉ Roentgenova 2
☎ 257 272 146/257 271 111
🚇 Bus 167 from Anděl Metro station to last stop

Canadian Medical Care (private clinic)
✚ Off map A4
✉ Veleslavínská 1
☎ 235 360 133
🚇 Tram 20, 26 to Nádraží Veleslavín

Language

"Czech is a Slavonic language, particularly closely related to Slovak and Polish, less so to Russian and the South Slav languages. Like them it has a complex grammar and many inflections. Pronunciation can be a problem for foreigners, but one bonus is that the language, unlike English, is pronounced as it is written, invariably with the stress on the first syllable of the word. Most Czechs dealing with visitors from abroad will speak at least some English, but it is always worthwhile learning a few stock phrases and becoming familiar with signs."

SHOPPING

How much is this? *Pomůžete mi, prosím?*

I'm looking for... *Kolik to stojí? Hledám...*

Where can I buy...? *Kde dostanu...?*

How much is this/that? *Kolik stojí tohle/tamto?*

When does the shop open/close?
Kdy tady otevíráte/zavíráte?

I'm just looking, thank you.
Děkují, jenom si prohlížím.

I'll take this. *Vezmu si to.*

Do you have anything less expensive/smaller/larger?
Máte něco levnějšího/menšího/většího?

Are the instructions included?
Jsou u toho pokyny pro uživatele?

Do you have a bag for this?
Máte na to tašku?

I'd like a kilo of... *Prosím kilo...*

This is the right size. *To je správná velikost.*

Do you have this in...? *Máte to v...?*

Is there a market? *Je tady někde trh/tržnic?*

USEFUL WORDS

yes *ano*
no *ne*
please *prosím*
thank you *děkují*
you're welcome *prosím/nemáte zač*
excuse me! *Promiňte!*
where *kde*
here *tady*
there *tam*
when *kdy*
now *ted'?*
later *později*
why *proč*
who *kdo*
may I/can I? *můžu?*

MONEY

Is there a bank/currency exchange office nearby? *Je tady někde blízko banka/směnárna?*

I'd like to change sterling/dollars into crowns (Kč, Czech currency)
Anglické libry/americké dolary za české koruny (Kč) prosím...

Can I use my credit card to withdraw cash?
Mohu vybírat hotovost na svoji kreditní kartu?

GETTING AROUND

Where is the train/bus station?
Kde je tady vlakové/autobusové nádraží?

Does this train/bus go to...?
Jede ten vlak/autobus do...?

Does this train/bus stop at...?
Staví ten vlak/autobus v...?

Please stop at the next stop.
Zastavte mi na další zastávce, prosím.

Where are we? *Kde jsme?*

Do I have to get off here? *Musím tady vystoupit?*

Where can I buy a ticket?
Kde si mohu koupit lístek?

Is this seat taken? *Je tady obsazeno?*

Where can I reserve a seat?
Kde si mohu rezervovat místo?

Please can I have a single/return ticket to...
Prosím jízdenku/zpáteční jízdenku do...

Where is the timetable? *Kde je jízdní řád?*

GENERAL QUERIES

Where is the tourist information office/desk, please?
Kde je informač středisko pro turisty, prosím?

Do you have a city map?
Máte mapu měesta?

Can you give me some information about...?
Promím informace o...?

What is the admission price?
Kolik stoji vstupné?

Are there guided tours?
Máte obhlídku s průvodcem?

Can we make reservations here?
Můžeme si tadyč?

How much is a ticket?
Kolík stojí lístek?

Where do they go?
Kam to jezdí?

DAYS OF THE WEEK

Monday *ponděli*
Tuesday *úterý*
Wednesday *středa*
Thursday *čtvrtek*
Friday *pátek*
Saturday *sobota*
Sunday *neděle*

Timeline

WHITE MOUNTAIN

In 1620 the Protestant army was routed at the Battle of White Mountain. Protestant leaders were executed in Old Town Square and Czechs who refused to reconvert to Catholicism emigrated en masse. A largely foreign nobility loyal to the Habsburgs, was installed,and Prague was beautified with churches and palaces. The court made Vienna its main seat and Prague became a sleepy provincial town.

FIRST REPUBLIC

Established in 1918, the First Czechoslovak Republic was a model democracy in many ways. However, it suffered from the insoluble problem of a large German minority.

From left: Jerome de Prague, burned as a heretic; Cathedral of St. Vitus; Jan Palach burned himself to death in political protest; John Lennon Wall; crosses representing executed noblemen; radical preacher Jan Hus

7th or 8th century AD Prague's legendary foundation by Princess Libuše.

10th century Trading settlements are set up in Lesser Town and Old Town.

1231 King Wenceslas I fortifies the Old Town with 13 towers, walls 12m (40ft) high and a moat (today's Na Příkopě, or Moat Street).

1253–78 Reign of King Otakar II, who extends and fortifies Lesser Town, inviting German merchants to settle there.

1415 Radical preacher Jan Hus is burned at the stake.

1576–1611 Reign of eccentric Emperor Rudolph II, patron of astrologers and alchemists.

1620 Battle of White Mountain.

1848 Austrian General Windischgrätz puts down a revolt led by students, but Czech nationalism continues to grow.

1914–18 Czechs are dragged against their will into World War I on the Austrian side. Many soldiers desert or join the Czechoslovak Legion fighting for the Allies.

1938 Czechoslovakia is forced to give up the Sudetenland to Nazi Germany.

1945–47 Expulsion of the 3 million German minority from Czechoslovakia.

1948 Communists, the most powerful party in the democratically elected goverment, stage a coup d'état. Stalinist repression follows.

1968 Prague Spring (▷ side panel).

1977 Dissident intellectuals sign Charter 77, a call for the government to apply the Helsinki Agreements of 1975. Many are harrassed and imprisoned.

1989 The Velvet Revolution. Václav Havel is elected president.

1993 Czechoslovakia splits into the independent states of Slovakia and the Czech Republic.

1999 The Czech Republic joins NATO.

2002 Catastrophic floods wreak havoc in Prague and throughout the country.

2003 Havel is replaced as president by former prime minister Václav Klaus.

2004 The Czech Republic joins the European Union.

2006 Electoral stalemate leaves Czechs without a government.

PRAGUE SPRING

In the 'Prague Spring' of 1968, Czechoslovakia's Communist party, under Alexander Dubček, promised to create 'Socialism with a human face'. Terrified at this prospect, the Soviet Union sent in tanks and took the government off to Moscow in chains. The last Soviet troops left in 1991.

PROTEKTORAT

In 1939, German troops marched into Prague, and Czechoslovakia became the 'Protectorate' of Bohemia-Moravia. Nazi rule was brutal, spectacularly so after the assassination of Reichsprotekor Heydrich, while the Holocaust brought to an end 1,000 years of Jewish history in the Czech lands. In May 1945, after the longest Nazi occupation in any European country, the people of Prague liberated their city and welcomed in the Red Army.

Index

Prague's
25 Best

WRITTEN BY Michael Ivory
DESIGN CONCEPT AND DESIGN WORK Kate Harling
COVER DESIGN Tigist Getachew
INDEXER Marie Lorimer
IMAGE RETOUCHING AND REPRO Michael Moody
EDITOR Bookwork Creative Associates
REVIEWING EDITOR Jacinta O'Halloran
SERIES EDITOR Paul Mitchell

Published in the United Kingdom by AA Publishing

ISBN 978-1-4000-1829-1

SIXTH EDITION

IMPORTANT TIP
Time inevitably brings changes, so always confirm prices, travel facts, and other perishable information when it matters. Although Fodor's cannot accept responsibility for errors, you can use this guide in the confidence that we have taken every care to ensure its accuracy.

SPECIAL SALES
This book is available for special discounts for bulk purchases for sales promotions or premiums. Special editions, including personalized covers, excerpts of existing books, and corporate imprints, can be created in large quantities for special needs. For more information, write to Special Markets/Premium Sales, 1745 Broadway, MD 6–2, New York, NY 10019 or email specialmarkets@randomhouse.com.

Colour separation by Keenes
Printed and bound by Leo, China
10 9 8 7 6 5 4 3 2 1

A03143

The Automobile Association would like to thank the following photographers, companies and picture libraries for their assistance in the preparation of this book.

Abbreviations for the picture credits are as follows – **(t)** top; **(b)** bottom; **(c)** centre; **(l)** left; **(r)** right; (AA) AA World Travel Library.

1 AA/C Sawyer; **2/3t** AA/C Sawyer; **4/5t** AA/ S McBride; **4** AA/J Wyand; **5** AA/S McBride; **6/7t** AA/S McBride; **6cl** AA/C Sawyer; **6cc** AA/J Wyand; **6cr** AA/S McBride; **6bl** AA/C Sawyer; **6bc** AA/J Smith; **6br** AA/S McBride; **7cl** AA/T Souter; **7ccl** AA/J Smith; **7ccr** AA/S McBride; **7cr** AA/C Sawyer; **7bl** AA/C Sawyer; **7bcl** AA/C Sawyer; **7bcr** AA/J Smith; **7br** AA/S McBride; **8/9t** AA/ S McBride; **10/11t** AA/S McBride; **10tr** AA/J Smith; **10ctr** AA/J Smith; **10/1c** AA/J Wyand; **10/1b** AA/J Smith; **11tl** AA/ S McBride; **11cl** AA/J Smith; **12/13t** AA/ S McBride; **13tl** Digitalvision; **13ctl** AA/J Smith; **13c** AA/J Wyand; **13cbl** AA/J Wyand; **13bl** AA/J Wyand; **14/5t** AA/ S McBride; **14tr** AA/J Smith; **14tcr** AA/J Wyand; **14bcr** AA/J Smith; **14br** AA/J Smith; **16/7t** AA/ S McBride; **16t** AA/J Smith; **16tc** AA/J Smith; **16bc** AA/ S McBride; **16b** AA/J Smith; **17t** AA/J Smith; **17tc** AA/J Wyand; **17bc** Image 100; **17b** AA/J Smith; **18t** AA/ S McBride; **18tc** AA/J Wyand; **18c** AA/C Sawyer; **18cb** AA/J Smith; **18b** AA/C Sawyer; **19(I)** AA/J Wyand; **19(II)** AA/J Smith; **19(III)** AA/J Wyand; **19(IV)** AA/C Sawyer; **19(V)** AA/C Sawyer; **20/1** AA/J Wyand; **24l** AA/J Smith; **24/5** AA/J Smith; **25r** AA/J Smith; **26l** AA/J Smith; **26tr** AA/J Smith; **26br** AA/J Smith/Jewish Museum, Prague; **26/7b**; AA/J Smith; **27tl** AA/ J Smith; **27bl** AA/ J Smith; **27r** AA/ J Smith; **28l** AA/J Wyand; **28/9t** AA/J Wyand; **28/9b** AA/S McBride; **29t** AA/J Wyand; **29bl** AA/C Sawyer; **29br** AA/S McBride; **30l** By Alphonse Mucha/Mucha Trust/BAL, AA/S McBride; **30c** AA/ S McBride; **30r** By Alphonse Mucha/Mucha Trust/BAL, AA/ S McBride; **31** AA/J Smith; **32l** AA/J Smith; **32/3tr** AA/J Wyand; **32br** AA/C Sawyer; **33t** AA/C Sawyer; **33bl** AA/S McBride; **33br** AA/J Smith; **34l** AA/J Smith; **34c** AA/J Smith; **34r** AA/J Smith; **35t** AA/J Wyand; **35bl** AA/J Smith; **35r** AA/J Smith; **36t** AA/J Wyand; **36bl** AA/S McBride; **36br** AA/J Wyand; **37** AA/J Smith; **38** AA/J Smith; **39** AA/J Smith; **40t** AA/J Wyand; **41** AA/J Smith; **42t** AA/S McBride; **42b** AA/J Wyand; **43** AA/J Wyand; **46l** By Alphonse Mucha/Mucha Trust/BAL, AA/J Smith; **46r** AA/S McBride; **47l** AA/C Sawyer; **47r** AA/J Smith; **48l** AA/J Wyand; **48r** AA/J Wyand; **49l** AA/S McBride; **49r** AA/J Smith; **50** AA/J Smith; **50/1t** AA/J Smith; **50/1b** AA/J Smith; **51t** AA/J Smith; **51bl** AA/J Smith; **51br** AA/S McBride; **52** AA/C Sawyer; **52/3t** AA/J Smith; **52/3b** AA/C Sawyer; **53** AA/J Wyand; **54t** AA/J Wyand; **54bl** AA/J Smith; **54br** AA/J Wyand; **55t** AA/J Wyand; **55bl** AA/J Wyand; 55br AA/J Smith; 56 AA/J Smith; 57 AA/J Smith; 58 Photodisc; 59 Photodisc; **60t** Digitalvision; **60b** AA/J Smith; **61** AA/J Smith; **62** AA/T Harris; **63** AA/J Smith; **66** AA/J Wyand; **67l** AA/C Sawyer; **67r** AA/J Wyand; **68** By Alphonse Mucha/Mucha Trust/BAL, AA/ J Wyand; **68/9t** AA/J Wyand; **68br** AA/ J Wyand; **69t** AA/C Sawyer; **68/9b** AA/S McBride; **69br** AA/C Sawyer; **70l** AA/S McBride; **70c** AA/S McBride; **70r** AA/S McBride; **71l** AA/J Smith; **71r** AA/J Smith; **72** AA/J Smith; **72/3t** AA/C Sawyer; **72/3b** AA/S McBride; **73t** AA/S McBride; **73bl** AA/S McBride; **73br** AA/S McBride; **74l** AA/J Wyand; **74/5** AA/S McBride; **75** AA/S McBride; **76t** AA/J Wyand; **76bl** AA/J Smith; **76br** AA/C Sawyer; **77t** AA/J Wyand; **77bl** AA/S McBride; **77br** AA/J Smith; **78** AA/J Smith; **79t** AA/J Smith; **79b** AA/J Smith; **80** AA/T Souter; **81** AA/T Souter; **84** AA/J Wyand; **84/5t** AA/S McBride; **84/5b** AA/T Souter; **85** AA/ J Wyand; **86l** AA/J Smith; **86c** AA/J Smith; **86r** AA/S McBride; **87l** AA/J Smith; **87r** AA/J Wyand; **88l** AA/C Sawyer; **88r** AA/J Wyand; **89t** AA/ J Wyand; **89b** AA/ J Wyand; **90** AA/ J Wyand; **90bl** AA/C Sawyer; **90br** AA/C Sawyer; **91** AA/J Smith; **92t** Photodisc; **92c** Brand X Pics; **93t** AA/C Sawyer; **94** AA/C Sawyer; **95** AA/C Sawyer; **98** AA/J Wyand; **98/9t** AA/ J Wyand; **98/9b** AA/C Sawyer; **99t** AA/J Wyand; **99bl** AA/C Sawyer; **99br** AA/C Sawyer; **100t** AA/J Smith; **100bl** AA/J Smith; **100br** AA/J Smith; **100/1t** AA/J Smith; **101bl** AA/J Smith; **101br** AA/J Smith; 102l AA/ J Wyand; 102r AA/ J Wyand; 103t AA/ J Wyand ; 103l AA/J Smith; 103r AA/ J Wyand ; **104t** AA/ J Wyand; **104bl** AA/ J Smith; **104br** AA/C Sawyer; **105t** AA/ J Wyand ; **105bl** AA/C Sawyer; **105bcl** AA/C Sawyer; **105bcr** AA/ J Wyand ; **105br** AA/ J Wyand; **106t** AA/ J Wyand; **106bl** AA/ J Wyand; **106br** AA/ J Wyand; **107** AA/ J Wyand; **108t** AA/C Sawyer; **108tr** AA/J Smith; **108tcr** AA/J Smith; **108c** AA/S McBride; **108br** AA/J Smith; **109t** AA/C Sawyer; **110/1t** AA/C Sawyer; **112** AA/C Sawyer; **113** AA/J Smith; **114/5** AA/ J Wyand; **116/7** AA/ J Wyand; **117** AA/J Smith; **118/9t** AA/J Wyand; **120/1** AA/ J Wyand; **121** AA/C Sawyer; **122/3t** AA/J Wyand; **122c** AA/ J Wyand; **124/5t** AA/ J Wyand; **124bl** AA; **124cb** AA; **124br** AA/J Wyand; **125bl** AA/ J Wyand; **125bc** AA/C Sawyer; **125br** AA.

Every effort has been made to trace the copyright holders, and we apologise in advance for any accidental errors. We would be happy to apply the corrections in the following edition of this publication.